We're here to help

What we learnt from saving a 140-year-old charity and how you can make your charity flourish.

SJOG is a UK based charity working to support people in need.

More details can be found at sjog.uk

Paul Bott, Lisa Alcorn, Jamie Mackrill and Leanne Welford have asserted their rights to be identified as the authors of this work in accordance with the Copyright, Designs and Patents Act 1988.

First published by SJOG in 2023: ISBN: 978-1-7395130-0-9

Every effort has been made to obtain the necessary permissions with reference to copyrighted material, both illustrative and quoted. We apologise for any omissions and will to be pleased to make the appropriate acknowledgements in any future edition.

SJOG does not have any control over, or any responsibility for, any author or third-party websites referred to in or on this book.

All income from the sale of this book goes to further the work of SJOG, a charity registered in England and Wales – RCN 1108428.

www.sjog.uk

ISBN: 978-1-7395130-1-6

Contents

1. **Why you should read this book**
2. **Charities and your role in their success**
3. **Leadership**
   What is it and your role in leading your organisation?
4. **Purpose**
   Why does your organisation need to exist?
6. **Getting started**
   What do you really know and how to know more
7. **Change is constant**
   How to manage big change and small change in your organisation
8. **Assurance**
   The role of governance in keeping your organisation from falling over
9. **Having a plan**
   Strategy and how to make sure that it makes a difference
10. **A Sound basis for success**
    The role of finance in keeping your organisation alive
11. **Good work**
    The role of people, and the importance of community in helping your organisation flourish
12. **Building better**
    The role of quality management systems in your long-term success
13. **A successful future**
    Building in innovation and opportunities from the very beginning
14. **Managing yourself**
    How to be comfortable with not being truly accomplished
15. **Reach out**
16. **Acknowledgements**
17. **Authors' bios**

Why you should read this book

No organisation has a right to exist

It's a shame, but organisations fail every day. Sometimes they fail catastrophically. Sometimes they fail in slow motion by just being ok, and in a competitive world when everyone else is moving forward towards good and outstanding, OK is just not OK.

We hope that this book will help you be better than OK; that it will help you avoid failure but most importantly that it will give you the greatest chance of success.

There are no guarantees in this world, but what you'll find here is the knowledge and experiences of a successful team who saved a 140-year-old charity from closure. More than just avoiding closure, they turned this charity into a thriving, multi award-winning organisation that can be of more help to more people each year, and that for us, is the key measure of success.

The four authors make up the senior team of SJOG. We came together four years ago, and we benefit from our differing backgrounds in business, academia and the charity sector. This diversity of thought helps us to make better decisions.

This is not a textbook (though we have two doctorates, an MBA and an MSc in management, between us); this book is instead our team sharing what they've learned with you and your team.

Any one of us could have written this book, but we wrote it together because there is a real benefit in having more than one voice, and just like the running an organisation, it's good to be able to turn to someone and say 'Well, what do you think?'.

We hope this book gives you and your team a bit of support. That it reinforces and builds on what you already know, and that it also offers a challenge to the way that you think about the work that you do.

We are hoping that this is just the start of a conversation between us and we are always happy to hear from people with questions, suggestions or just because you want to get in touch. Email paulbott@sjog.org.uk, leannewelford@sjog.org.uk, lisaalcorn@sjog.org.uk, and jamiemackrill@sjog.org.uk

The SJOG context

Though we come from a range of backgrounds, the four of us came together at SJOG around the end of 2018. At this point the charity was in a pickle. It had lost its way.

SJOG can trace its roots in the UK back to 1880. By 2012 it had grown to become a successful charity delivering £25million of services and had built a healthy £9million in reserves, but then it had all gone wrong, not suddenly, but gradually over a number of years.

Services were closed and of the 26 services that remained, 25 of them were running at a deficit. The charity covered these operating losses by dipping into the reserves. By 2018, the charity had shrunk to an operational income of £15million and all of its reserves were spent.

The trustees knew that something had to change; they recruited a new chief executive, who then recruited a new senior team. When we arrived, the charity was losing £35,000 a week. The board of trustees gave the new senior team 12 months, and if a turnaround couldn't be enacted in that time, then the charity would close.

The challenges were not just financial. Services were rated by our regulator as inadequate or requiring improvement and staff turnover stood at 42% a year. There were legal issues and relationships with funders were damaged.

The charity had a feel that it needed some love. Even from the outside, you could see this. The website was old fashioned and limited, the numbers in the annual reports showed the financial decline, and the narrative in the public reports was cut and pasted from one year to the next.

Conversations with the trustees showed that they had strong values and this was repeated in meetings with colleagues across the organisation. Visiting all of our services in our first three months, we listened to our colleagues and saw that the quality of the interactions between the people working in the charity and the people that we are here to support were really good, but they just weren't capturing this evidence to show how good they were.

At its heart there was a good charity here, but where people were succeeding, they were doing this in spite of the charity rather than because of the charity's support.

In our visits we were honest with our colleagues about the state we found ourselves in and the challenges we faced. They shared with us what was important to them, and we put trust in our colleagues, giving them the support and structures so that they could be involved in turning the charity's performance around.

Together we built a strategy, a plan to help us to get from where we were to where we wanted to be, and as we started to deliver on this, we built trust by doing what we said we would do.

The senior team were great, and we met at least weekly to make sure progress was being made in each of our areas, but it's a key point that there's always been great people working in the charity. It's all of us pulling in the same direction that changed the fortunes of the charity.

Within a year we posted a surplus and raised our quality ratings. Within two years all services were rated 'Good' or 'Outstanding' by our external regulator, and we had added 10 new services and rebuilt our reserves to sensible levels.

It was a lot of work and quality work that was recognised in national awards as the 'Charity Change Project of the Year'. The charity also went from almost closing to being shortlisted as the Charity of the Year within a 2-year window.

What's really important is to restate that we added just a few new colleagues. Most of the people who were in the failing charity were also in the award-winning charity, so, what's the difference?

The difference was that we talked and most importantly listened to the people who really understood what was going on. We treated our colleagues with respect and brought in a little expertise to provide direction and to align and evidence their work. Most of all though we helped our colleagues to rediscover their sense of ambition for the charity.

It's our colleagues who stuck with it during the difficult times who should be most applauded for the turnaround. They stayed and worked even when things weren't going right, because their focus was always that 'We're here to help'.

There will be more stories in this book about what was done to turn around the charity and what we learned from this. Whilst this book is about how to turnaround an organisation, it's also about how you can shape your organisation so that it can be of more help and has the greatest chance of success of delivering on its purpose.

There is a lot of information in the book that we've developed ourselves, some that we've adapted and adopted from work in the sector, and there's also some of our favourite theories and information from leaders in the third sector and business. We've gathered, collated and added a sprinkling of learning that is entirely new. Hopefully it will be of help so read on!

Charities and your role in their success

What you will find here:

- Charities - what are they?
- Your purpose

Making a start

Charities are brilliant things and helping them to flourish is a worthwhile endeavour and that's what this book is about. However, charities are just organisations for social benefit and so the learning contained in this book will be useful to anyone working in any organisation, but our experience is as a team of people who run an award-winning flourishing charity.

Charities in the UK

If you ask the man or women in the street about charities, then the pervading picture will be that of a group of people, well-meaning, and trying to do well, but probably not as effective as 'real' businesses in actually getting stuff done.

There may be a greater number of idealists in the charity sector, beard wearers who knit their own muesli, but that's not the whole story. The charity sector is a diverse collection of 169,000 organisations and richer for it.

To put this in some kind of perspective, the charity sector employs almost one million people, that's about 3% of the workforce of England and Wales. Through reserves and endowments, it owns 2% of the stock market, and each year the charity sector spends £60 billion on public good.

In terms of scale, if all of the police officers in England and Wales and those in the Fire Service were added to all of the people in the Army, Navy and Royal Air Force, they would still be smaller than the charity sector.

The charity sector is important both to the economic wealth of the UK, but most important is its role in meeting needs not met elsewhere. The charity sector builds communities and ensures that we live in a country that is fair, and supports everyone to contribute their talents, even those at the very margins.

Charities are important. Initially I thought my role in charities was to change the world for the better. It is, but I think now that the most important role of charities is to change the world of the people we support for the better, and that's a subtle but important difference.

You're it!

I've never started with a blank piece of paper. Every organisation I have worked in, volunteered in and supported was already up and running. Each had an established way of working, a track record, a culture. In each there were great things and some things that were less great. There was always room to grow, to make positive changes and help make the organisation just a bit better at delivering on their purpose.

As a leader, your role is to make your organisation successful. There isn't another group of people sat in another room who are also doing this. You are it. You are responsible and it's down to you to do all you can to navigate the changing environment.

This responsibility can be scary, but hopefully it leads to action rather than paralysis, as the only way to make your organisation successful is to start doing.

There will be doubts along the way and a worry that you might not be up to it. We all have those (and it's why we have a whole chapter on how to manage yourself, so that you can be a more confident leader) but the success of your charity will depend on you being comfortable with the role you have and with a degree of risk. That includes not knowing whether this is going to work out.

In over 25 years in the charity sector, I've seen people do amazing things, but I've been in too many meetings where a group of people who can do nothing, agree that nothing can be done.

I have spoken with people running charities who really believe that they were victims of circumstance. That the reason that the charity was failing was because they were in a sector that was in terminal decline and that they were managing that decline. That the commissioners of services didn't pay enough, or even that the comissioners didn't like them.

Let's deal with this now, the world will continue to change around you. You either navigate successfully through those changes or you don't. As for comissioners of services, they don't care about you. It's not about like or not like. They just want you to do a good job.

So as the world continues to change, it's up to you to find the way forward.

You are responsible and you should be held accountable for the success of your charity, but the good news is that you have the ability to make changes and make things better rather than waiting for things to get better. Don't wait. Get started.

If you've picked up this book, then you are interested in how to make your organisation better. It might be on the brink of collapse, have lost its way, or it might just need a tweak to make it truly brilliant.

In taking that next step, the received wisdom is that you first work out where you are now and where you want to get to.

The great thing about working for a charity is that you already have a framework. Your charity will already be working towards a goal and so whilst your exact path might not be plotted, your direction of travel should be established.

> ### Reflection
> - Charities are brilliant things and helping them to flourish is a worthwhile endeavour.
> - As a leader it is your role to give your organisation the greatest chance of being successful.

Leadership

What is it and your role in leading your organisation

What you will find here:

- The art of leadership
- The leadership top 10
- The Bananarama principle

The art of leadership

I used to worry about being a leader, and whether I was a leader or just good at managing people and projects.

I've met some great leaders and people who thought they were great leaders but really weren't. I didn't want to be in that latter category, so I tried to work out what was the difference between leadership and management. I read lots of things like management is a science and leadership is an art, and thought 'OK, but what do I do with that?'.

I read books on leadership, and there are so many of varied worth - really good pieces by thinkers like Peter Drucker and books that I found less useful, that encourage you to 'Lead like Moses', and 'The Shakespearean Leader'. I kid you not and these are real books and were included in the great article from Rob Goffey and Gareth Jones called 'Why should anyone be led by you' which is a simply brilliant title for an article on leadership and a question that I've often asked myself.

I've come to the conclusion that it is a question which is not for me to answer. If people follow you then you are their leader, if they don't then you are not. You can influence this, but they get to decide, you don't.

I'm not sure how much of my reading I actually held on to. I think you have to work it out as you go along. You work out what kind of leader you are going to be, and then you try to be a bit better at what you do and the way that you do it. Yes, I can see the irony in writing about leadership and saying that books on leadership are not useful, but we'll plough on.

My learning on leadership is as likely to come from the kids in the playground, or from plays, or TV.

My daughter has just discovered Grey's Anatomy and is working her way through the numerous series of the hospital drama. For those of you not familiar with Grey's, the drama shows the interconnected lives of surgeons working in the same hospital. It shows the challenges in their relationships and the chaos of their private lives as well as leading teams in the operating theatres working to save someone's life.

The interesting thing that I take away from this is that leaders are people. Their private lives might be a mess, but they still turn up for work where sometimes they have astounding successes, sometimes abject failures, but most of the time they come somewhere between the two.

So, what is leadership?

Leadership for me isn't about guaranteeing success, and it's definitely not about prohibiting failure, but it is about creating an environment where our colleagues can thrive, and we have the greatest chance of successfully delivering on our purpose.

The key thing that I've learnt is that leadership is about helping people get somewhere; that might be to deliver on a charitable purpose; to make squillions in private industry; or to keep the peace in an unstable area of the world. (You decide where you spend your energy!)

To structure that a bit better, it's about:

1. being clear about why we are here, what our purpose is;
2. setting expectations about what we are going to do to achieve that purpose;
3. giving people the tools, training and support so that they can succeed, and then...
4. getting out of their way as they deliver;
5. ...but being ready to step in if more support is needed.

How do I become a leader?

As far as I can tell there is no single recipe for being a leader. Each of the organisations that I've worked in has been different, every team that I've been in has been different, and the leadership that they needed has also been different.

I've worked with loose groups who are used to working on their own. Leadership for this group has just been about coordinating their activities.

I've worked with teams of young people who need more guidance and bring levels of enthusiasm and energy, lots of passion and little experience. Leadership for this group has been more about crowd control and repeatedly bringing them back to the task in hand.

I've also worked with troubled teams who were dysfunctional because of the relationships in the team. Where I was unsuccessful in dealing with this through mediation, we ended up splitting up the team. It was ugly; people lost their jobs but the positive that came from this was that we built a new team that was much more effective at doing what it needed to do. If you can't change the people, change the people.

Working out where you want to go, and helping people to get there will sometimes need you to make difficult decisions, and I've always found that when this is the case, then focus on delivering on the purpose of the charity.

Leadership top 10

In writing this book I thought about what I would have find useful to have when I was starting out, and to remind myself of today. Here's my top 10.

1. **Be clear about what you are trying to achieve**
   It all comes back to purpose. If you understand why you are here and what you are trying to achieve, then that brings a focus to all of your decisions.

2. **Do stuff**
   Get stuff done. Teams exist for a purpose. So do it, don't just talk about it, and measure the impact you are having along the way so that you can show that you've done stuff that actually delivers on what you are trying to achieve. Turn thinking into doing.

3. **Decide what you will tolerate**
   You set the standards for the organisation. You decide what will be tolerated, and what you tolerate, you condone. I believe everyone wants to do a good job, but we need to know what good looks like,

what the expectation is. We do this by sharing examples of good and outstanding pieces of work. We say to people, "Ok! This is what we need to aim for" and once people have a target then they can work towards it.

4. **You're it**

    As leaders we help and develop people, we change them by providing guidance and support, but if they won't grow and develop, or are not willing to try, or in some cases if they don't have the capability, then we put the good of the charity above the individual. That might mean having to part company and change the people in the team. It's never comfortable saying goodbye to people, but you do need to be courageous enough to have the difficult conversations, so that you can have the best chance of successfully delivering on our purpose.

5. **…but you are not 'IT'**

    The danger is that when you are 'in charge' that people start to treat you like you are important, and the danger is that you start to act that you believe you are important. You are not 'IT.' This is not about you; this is about delivering on the purpose of the charity, and you my friend are just a cog in that particular machine. Be humble.

6. **You are a human being**

    Be you, bring all of yourself to work, and be comfortable with the fact that you are who you are, with your own skills and shortfalls. You need to know yourself so that you can find other members of your team who make up for your shortfalls.

7. **You are not Google**

    Be comfortable not to know everything. This one took me a long time to learn. You are human, not Google. Admit when you don't know stuff, and then find a way to find out.

8. **…but you need to know stuff**

    Know why you are in the room. It might be that you have a better understanding of the gestalt (see page 55). It might be that you are needed to referee, or to help the team arrive at a decision, or to give permission for a course of action. Whatever it is you need to know, know that, and how to do that.

9. **You are not alone**

    Can you be a leader if there is no one else? Leadership implies that there is at least one other person, and so you don't have to do all the work yourself. Lead but don't be afraid to get involved. Leading by doing is great, but don't do it all. Do it with people not for people.

10. **Rely on others**

    Collectively your team knows more than you do. They can generate more ideas and achieve more. Help them by creating an environment where they can flourish and bring all of their genius to work.

    Ask for help. That might be with a specific problem, or even better find yourself a mentor, someone who has found their own way of doing things and who you can use as a sounding board as you find your own way.

Bonus Time

The underlying current in all of this is what Robert K. Greenleaf called 'servant leadership'. Being a leader is not about being in power, or making all of the decisions but instead Greenleaf, writing back in the 1970s stated that a leader should focus on the following question:

"Do those served grow as persons? Do they, while being served, become healthier, wiser, freer, more autonomous, more likely themselves to become servants?"

In SJOG this is expressed simply within our core value of Hospitality; every day we say 'Come in, you are most welcome, how can I be of help?'

To capture that simply, point number 11 in our leadership top 10 would be.

11. **Be of help**

The Bananarama principle

Bananarama were one of the most successful girl groups ever to grace the UK pop charts. Amongst their numerous hits was 'It ain't what you do it's the way that you do it.' I buy into this wholeheartedly. As a leader you set the tone.

Now, I believe in the power of nice. If you are kind and considerate to the people around you then this is reflected in the team, in their interactions, and the interactions of the people that they interact with until it becomes 'the way that we do things around here'.

'The way we do things around here' is my favourite definition of 'culture'.

Culture is established over time. It isn't one thing, or even consistent across an organisation, but it is determined by the little things that you do every day. Do you say please every time you ask someone for something, even in an email, or do you not? Do you remember to say thank you or well done? When someone has done something silly, do you pause and wonder why they did it, and how you can ask them what they think of what has happened, or do you plough in and make your displeasure known?

...and at this point I look at tip number 5.

I'm aware of trying to be positive, setting the tone, and being aware of positional power. that even a small rebuke may have more impact if it comes from the chief executive, but like everyone else there are times when I'm grumpy, or tired, or at the end of my tether, and I start to focus too much on me and at this point and once again I remind myself to refocus on tip number 5 to remind myself that it's not about me.

Just as we cut ourselves a break and give ourselves the chance to refocus, we need to allow for others to be human too and help them to refocus. Leadership is about helping people get somewhere.

Communities

Organisations are communities. Every member of that community will be adding something to their community and should receive something back. That might just be a salary but hopefully it's more than that; a sense of belonging; a feeling of contributing; of being important and being valued.

There's a phrase that I think captures this perfectly: 'From each according to their ability. To each according to their need'. I know it has political connotations but taken on its own merit, it captures the interdependencies of communities, and organisations are communities.

We all have things we need help with; we all have things that we can contribute, even if it is only a smile or a thank you. That's what makes community, both giving and receiving and when we use all the talents of the people in our communities to get stuff done, then it's a richer experience.

As a leader of a community you have a special role, but before you can lead a community you have to be part of the community and we're back at tip 5.

Being a part and apart

We all want to belong.

When I first arrived in the charity, I spent some time getting to know it by talking with people and reading the various papers and documents that told me what the charity did and what its purpose was, and that was summarised as 'We are here to meet need where we find it'.

The problem I had was that 'need' signals that there is a deficit, so effectively we are dealing with a problem. I'd much rather be helping to build something positive and so we asked the question to the people that work and are served by the charity 'What makes your life worthwhile?'

Dr Jamie undertook the research and captured it all in a research document that is supported by academic thinking (there's more on this in the chapter on strategy called 'Having a Plan'), but the answers came into three main areas.

- **Having a purpose** - A reason to get out of bed in the morning. This might be taking care of a cat or searching for a cure for cancer. The purpose is not important, having one is.

- **Belonging** - Having someone who is important to you, and to whom you are important.

- **Health** - Physical, mental and emotional health so you can do the things that are important to you.

Fig 1. A life worthwhile

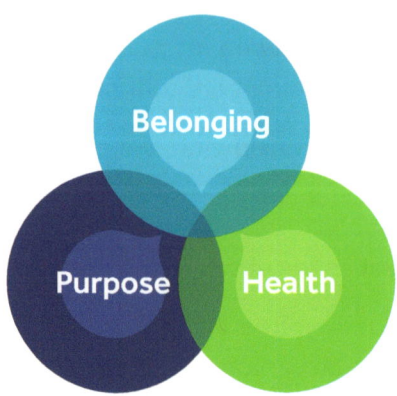

We all want to belong, but as a leader you need to be part of the community and apart.

I trained as a schoolteacher originally. As a 19 year old, just going into my first teaching practice, I was told to be friendly but to remember that the pupils, who were only a few years younger than I, were not my friends. This was my introduction to the idea of professional detachment. Sometimes we need to be able to take a step back to really take in the view of what's going on.

I have a friend who is a doctor and he tells a similar story. When people go to see their doctor, they want someone who has a professional interest in what is going on with their health. What they don't want is the same reaction that they get from their friends, 'Oh you have a rash that's terrible… and that is really horrible!'

The great thing about people is that we are complex and have the ability to be warm and caring, but still maintain the professionalism that is so important. As I say the challenge for any leader is to be a part but also apart.

Being a leader isn't a popularity contest (unless of course you are a political leader, in which case getting the job is the biggest popularity contest!). Goffey and Jones who we spoke about earlier stress the importance of separateness, and that inspirational leaders use this separateness to motivate others. They also warn of being too aloof, too much differentiation so that people stop following you. Being warm, caring and professional is a tightrope but fortunately you are a complex and capable person and can find your own level.

Be friendly to your colleagues and supportive of them. Whilst colleagues are with us we will do all that we can for them, but I hold on to the fact that colleagues are only in the charity as long as they are of benefit to delivering on the purpose, or until they choose to move on.

We support our colleagues, providing opportunities to learn and hopefully use this role to get where they want to in life. We're supportive of personal aspirations and we're friendly, but tell me honestly what was the name of the colleague that you sat next to five years ago? What was their brother's name or their child's? The point I'm making is that we have professional relationships, we are a friendly organisation and have lots of laughter and fun in the charity, but these are professional relationships and colleagues are not your friends.

...and having said that some of the greatest friendships in my life have come through work.

Elsewhere in the book we talk about the fact that running a charity is a team sport. You need buddies, either within or outside of your charity, but I've purposefully differentiated between friends and buddies. Just remember it's hard to put the purpose first and fire a friend. You've been warned. Tread carefully.

> ## Reflection
>
> The key role as a leader is to create an environment where your colleagues can thrive.
>
> Give people the tools, training and support to develop and grow but if you can't change the people, change the people.
>
> Be clear about what your organisational purpose is, and use that as the underpinning of all decisions.

References

Goffey, R. and Jones, G (2000). Why Should Anyone Be Led by You? Harvard Business Review. September 2000.

Greenleaf, R. K. (2002).Servant Leadership: A Journey into the Nature of Legitimate Power and Greatness (25th anniversary ed.). New York: Paulist Press.

Mackrill, J. (2019). A Life Worthwhile.

Purpose

Why does your organisation need to exist?

What you will find here:

- The what and how of charitable purpose
- Focus

Charitable purpose

All charities exist for a purpose, and the purpose of any charity, and therefore the people working in the charity, is to deliver public benefit.

That focus on public benefit was established over 400 years ago in the preamble of the Statute of Elizabeth, more correctly known as the Charitable Uses Act of 1601, which set out both the first requirement of public benefit and a list of charitable purposes.

> 'Relief of the aged, impotent, and poor people; maintenance of sick and maimed soldiers and mariners, schools of learning, free schools, and scholars in universities, repair of bridges, ports, havens, causeways, churches, sea banks, and highways, education and preferment of orphans, for or towards relief of stock, or maintenance for houses of correction, marriages of poor maids, supportation, aid, and help of young tradesmen, handicraftsmen, and persons decayed, relief or redemption of prisoners or captives, aide or ease of any poor inhabitants concerning payments of fifteens, setting out soldiers of soldiers and other taxes'.

The world, our use of language and the law has changed a little since then, but the latest Charities Act still sets out the definition of what purposes a charity must have to be defined as a charity. Those purposes are not very far at all from the 1601 definitions, though animals now get a mention.

The thirteen areas are:

1. The prevention or relief of poverty
2. The advancement of education
3. The advancement of religion
4. The advancement of health or the saving of lives
5. The advancement of citizenship or community development

6. The advancement of the arts, culture, heritage, or science
7. The advancement of amateur sport
8. The advancement of human rights, conflict resolution or reconciliation or the promotion of religious or racial harmony or equality and diversity
9. The advancement of environmental protection or improvement
10. The relief of those in need, by reason of youth, age, ill-health, disability, financial hardship or other disadvantage
11. The advancement of animal welfare
12. The promotion of the efficiency of the armed forces of the Crown, or of the efficiency of the police, fire and rescue services or ambulance services. And finally, the vaguest...
13. Any other charitable purposes

As a charity you exist to fulfil a purpose and that purpose is more than just to continue to exist. As a charity or social business your purpose is to do good for your community, whether that is a geographic community or a community of people with a shared interest or need.

Everything that you do within your charity, when raising money, delivering services, employing people, training, paying bills, are important only in so much as they help you deliver on that purpose.

The other learning to take away from this is that charities exist within a legal framework that defines what you can and can't do, but we'll cover this more in the Assurance chapter.

Your purpose, the 'what' and the 'how'

There are two important facets to purpose: 'The What' and 'The How'.

'The What' is easy to determine, it will be in the governing document for your charity. These are sometimes referred to as the 'mem and arts' or more formally known as the Articles of Association. These set out in black and white why your organisation exists. If you don't know where yours is, and you are a charity based in England and Wales, then this will be listed on the charity commission website.

Even if you think you know why your charity exists go and check. Read the governing documents as they are a fantastic resource. Not only will they tell you what your purpose is, they will also say what rules are in place for making decisions.

Some governing documents are drawn really tightly; some are as wide ranging as 'supporting the poor at home and around the world.' Whatever is in your objects is the scope of your work. This is what you were created to do.

In a previous role I was told that the charity was created to support people with sight loss. That was what it said on the website, that was what everyone I asked told me, and they wholeheartedly believed it, but that's not what we were established for. Our governing documents said that we were a charity for 'people affected by sight loss', which is similar but subtly different.

This difference opened up a whole new range of services for the parents of children with sight loss, and support for the families and carers of people who had been told they were losing their sight or had recently lost their sight.

'The How' is the interesting bit and just to be clear, there's a difference between what your purpose is, and how you deliver it.

The stated purpose of your charity may be 'the support of the elderly' but how you choose to do that, through grant giving, supper clubs, IT courses, providing transport, podiatry, providing support animals or through an over 50s skydiving club, is to up to you (or more accurately up to your trustees).

The 'How' of purpose is so important. It should define the decisions you make, what you say 'yes' to and just as importantly what you say 'no' to. In terms of defining this, I'd say:

"Work on it. Write it down. Share it."

It will help to set the agenda and the direction that the charity is going to take.

The example I carry with me is not actually a charity, but an example of a company created with a social purpose, the John Lewis Partnership.

John Spedan Lewis, the man who created the John Lewis Partnership, wrote down the principles over 100 years ago.

> "The first principle and the ultimate purpose of the Partnership is the happiness of all its members, through their worthwhile and satisfying employment in a successful business."

There's someone who knows what success looks like, and he spells out both 'The What' – 'the happiness of its members', and 'The How' – 'through their worthwhile and satisfying employment in a successful business'. Brilliant!

The other thing about 'The What' and The How' of John Lewis is that there is an ambition, expressed here in being a successful business.

When you set your 'What' and your 'How', please avoid being pedestrian stating what you do now, be ambitious for the people and the causes that you support.

Two more historical examples for you of truly excellent explanations of purpose are from the ESB and Lever Brothers.

In the 1880s, the Lever brothers were launching the first packaged laundry soap 'Sunlight Household Soap' and it was a runaway success. What's of more interest to us though is that they thought about and wrote down their purpose, which was;

> "Doing well by doing good."

The fact that this may have been borrowed by Benjamin Franklin is secondary. They had a purpose and expressed it concisely. The company the Lever brothers established still makes soap powder today but has grown into the international conglomerate Unilever. They've moved away from 'doing well by doing good' and now express their purpose as the much less concise and significantly blander 'Making Sustainable Living Commonplace'.

The third and final example that I'd like to draw your attention to is also historical. In the 1920s, the Irish electricity generator ESB, was bringing electricity to communities across Ireland, with the stated purpose of:

> "Lightening human burdens, brightening human lives."

I think it's brilliant; both in its structure; in its economy; and in its sentiment.

What gets me is that whilst this works brilliantly for an electric company, it would work equally well for a charity and would reflect all the excellent work done in lightening human burden and brightening human lives.

In defining your purpose, it's not about coming up with a strapline, or a vision or a mission statement. It's something else. If it's short then that helps, but what is more important is that it is memorable. The first principle of the John Lewis Partnership comes in at 27 words, hardly snappy, and it's not its strapline, which for many years was 'Never knowingly undersold'.

Your purpose is your core, the thing that defines everything that you do. For SJOG we capture this as: 'We're here to help'.

We're here to help

The story of how we got to 'We're here to help' goes back to when I joined the charity.

I'd read the annual reports, spoken to the team, and had started a tour of all of our services to get a feel for what was at the heart of the charity, to try and understand what we really did, and the way that we did it.

It was a tough time, the charity was losing money hand over fist and arriving as the new CEO, I knew that if we couldn't turn the charity around in 12 months then it would close, which would impact on each of our 400 colleagues and I felt that responsibility keenly.

Things were so tight that at one point if we hadn't received a legacy in the middle of the month, then we wouldn't have had enough funds to make payroll at the end of the month.

Whilst on my tour, I was talking with a support worker in one of our services about the challenges, the things that didn't work, and after a deep breath she leapt into a long list of issues around payments for contractors, outdated IT, lack of support and a disconnect between how we presented ourselves and how things were on the ground. After such a long list I asked her why she stuck with it, and she replied, "Because, we are here to help."

What I love about that, is that she knew what the purpose of the charity was, she felt it, and she saw it every day in her work, and though the words used elsewhere were different, the impetus was the same.

We didn't need a brand consultancy to come and package that for us, we just needed to listen to the people who knew the charity best, our colleagues.

Fig 2. We're here to help - strategy review

Staying on purpose

Having looked at what your charity's purpose actually is, and how you are going to deliver this, you might also have an idea of what your charity is doing at the moment that doesn't quite fit with the purpose.

Over time a charity changes, it develops pet projects, or chases funding that 'kind of' fits with what it does. These will need reviewing.

If you're not quite sure whether something fits or not, then that's telling you something.

When you sail, you have to pay attention to the conditions, what's going on with the sea, and most importantly what's going on with the wind. It's the wind that provides the power by pushing on the sail. When the wind is strong, there is a danger that the boat will be tipped over. Rather than staying on the shore, there are things that you can do when the wind is strong; you can reef your sail. Reefing your sail is reducing the size of the sail by rolling it or folding it to the mast or the boom. A smaller sail means less surface area for the wind to push against, which means less force pushing your boat over.

So, if you're looking at the weather and thinking do I need to reef today, the rule that novice sailors are taught is that if you are asking the question 'Do I need to reef?', then you need to reef.

I shared this story with a colleague who said they have a similar rule about using the bathroom before you leave the house. If you're asking, you need to go.

The same applies to those things that you do that don't quite fit with your purpose. If you are not sure about whether you need to stop doing these things, then you need to stop doing these things, but before you make the decision it's worth checking that what you think you know is actually right by really getting to know your charity and there's more on this in the next chapter.

Share your purpose

Once you are clear on what your purpose is, and you can express it simply, then share it. Make sure that it's shared often within your organisation, and repeat it often, yes repeat it often. By doing so, you give your colleagues the tools to talk about the charity, to explain what it is they do, and why they do it.

Questions to ask yourself

- What is the actual purpose of our charity, as listed in our governing documents?
- How do we deliver on that purpose?
- What do we do that doesn't fit with that purpose?
- Where are the gaps where we could be doing more?
- Can we express our purpose simply so that our colleagues can share it?

> **Reflection**
> - It's all about purpose.
> - There is a difference between the 'what' and 'how' of purpose.
> - ...and if you only take one thing from this book - it's all about purpose.

References

Charitable Uses Act of 1601 (known as the Statute of Elizabeth) (43 Eliz I, c.4) The Charities Act 2022 .London: HMSO.

Electric Generations 2017 ESB Advertising the early years. Cited https://electricgenerations.wordpress.com/2017/06/19/esb-advertising

John Lewis (2023) How we run our business today: The John Lewis Memory store. https://jlpmemorystore.org.uk/content/resources/people-and-partners/run-business-today

NCVS 2022 UK Civil Society Almanac 2022. Data. Trends. Insights (published October 2022)

Unilever (2020) 90 Years of doing good. Why companies with purpose last https://www.unilever.eo.uk/news/2020/90-years-of-doing-good-why-companies-with-purpose-last/

Getting started

What you really know and
how to know more

What you will find here:

- Understanding your charity
- People, quality and money
- Getting the 'smell of the place'
- Defining what success means to you

Getting to know you

Whether for good or for evil we live in the information age. Don't get me wrong, I love search engines; they help me to find information relating to absolutely any subject that I want to know about. On the downside quickly typing 'charity' into Google has just given me 'About 526,000,000 results in (0.79 seconds)'.

That's like looking for the right grain of sand on a long beach. Too much information. What I want is the right piece of information in my hand when I need it, not to know that somewhere, amongst 526,000,000 pieces of information is the piece that I'm looking for.

In the UK there used to be a TV advert for an insurance company which was set at a beach. In it a dad stands in a hole on the beach with a child's bucket and spade. He turns to his little son and says, "Where did you say you buried daddy's car keys?" to which his son replies emphatically, "I told you, they're in the sand."

I'm sure that in the response from Google all of the information will be in there, but the question is not where you find information, but where are the important nuggets of information amongst those 526,000,000 grains that will help you to understand where your charity is.

Knowing where to start digging to uncover the important bits is important, and I'd suggest that in any organisation the key information is around people, quality and money. We'll start with money.

Money

Unless you're like Leanne, our chief finance officer, managing finances is probably not the main reason in choosing to work for a charitable organisation (and knowing Leanne that's not her main driver either), but everyone should understand the money.

If you can earn a salary and pay your household bills, then you can understand the basics of money in a charity. Understanding the finances is important to the financial health of the charity and its financial health will determine how successful you are in delivering your purpose in the long term.

We'll walk through this. It's simpler than you think, and we'll try not to make this feel like double maths.

Are we financially healthy?

Financial health is like physical health, it's not important other than it allows us to do all the things that we want to in life.

Unless we are financially healthy, we can't deliver on our purpose in the long term.

I know that most people would rather focus on the 'doing' than the finances, but this is important and so sometimes you have to do what I once overheard someone refer to 'pulling your big girl pants on and just get on with it'.

Finding out how healthy you are requires just a little work, and the best place to start is with your financial accounts. If you can't find yours then they can be downloaded from the Charity Commission website. You'll need the accounts for the past three years.

In understanding how well your organisation is doing financially and the trend of the charity, the Trustees Annual Reports are the single most useful source of information.

Let's do this step by step.

Ignore the text initially, as it will have been polished to present the best version of what's gone on in the year, and skip right to auditor's comments. This will highlight whether the auditor had any concerns and what they might be. As you build your understanding of the charity, it's always useful to have another opinion. It's better if this is an expert opinion and best if it's an external expert opinion.

We'll start gently with just three numbers to start to understand how financially healthy your charity is.

1. How much you have coming in.
2. How much money you have going out.
3. How much savings you have to act as a buffer when life throws you a surprise.

   So far so simple.

To find these three numbers in your accounts skip straight to the first two pages of the financial reports. These will be snappily titled: 'STATEMENT OF FINANCIAL ACTIVITIES INCLUDING INCOME AND EXPENDITURE ACCOUNT'.

The first number you are looking for is TOTAL INCOME. This is how much money you have coming in.

The next number we are looking for is titled TOTAL RESOURCES EXPENDED. This is how much money you have going out. The difference between these will either be recorded as a surplus or deficit. If it is in brackets, it's a deficit and tells you that you are spending more money then you have coming in.

The final number you need for a snapshot of how financially healthy your charity is, is the amount of savings that you have and you will find this on the balance sheet.

The balance sheet will be the next page and it tells you how many assets the organisation has, how much is tied up in buildings and equipment, and how much is available in cash. The number you are looking for here is TOTAL ASSETS LESS CURRENT LIABILITIES. This is how much savings you have to act as a buffer, and how many assets you have that you could, potentially, borrow on.

Record these numbers in the simple table we've provided below. Then do it again for each of the four years (each accounts give you the current and previous years- so three sets of accounts give four years of numbers).

Fig 3. Understanding accounts

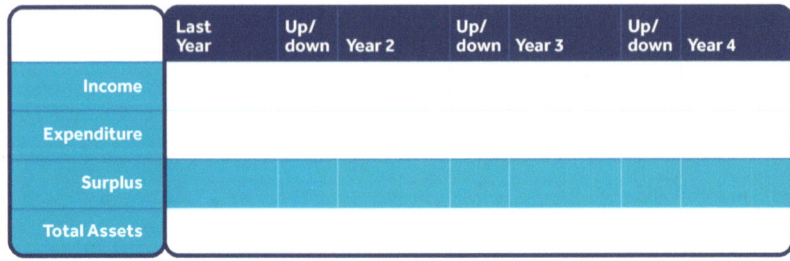

You'll see we've snuck a fourth number into the table - surplus. This is just the total income minus the total expenditure and we'll come back to this later.

Now that you have your numbers, what you are looking for is the story behind the numbers. Look across the years at the numbers comparing with the previous year and draw an arrow up or down beside it to show the movement from the previous year.

Simply if the charity income is going up then the charity's income is growing. If the numbers are going down then the charity's income is shrinking. It is the trend that we're looking for here.

Likewise, the expenditure will tell you how fast costs are growing, and whether increased income has led to more activity.

Hopefully there will be a surplus in each of the years. If you want to get a bit fancier then the percentage of surplus to income will give you an idea of whether it's becoming more difficult to cover your costs.

For assets, the trend to look for is whether there is a decline or growth in assets over the years.

In the book we have a whole chapter on finances, please don't skip this for three very important reasons:

1. Leanne worked extremely hard on this;
2. Leanne and her team were the Charity Finance Team of the Year, so you'd be passing up external expert advice and finally, and most importantly;
3. It's important to the success of your charity.

For the moment though you have a picture how the charity has worked over the past four years, whether it's thriving, surviving or declining.

What you've worked through here is a very quick process that will give an indication of the financial health of your charity, but the caveat here is that it's only an indication.

We'll talk about the importance of using indicators later in the book. Indicators are just that, they are not the story, but they tell you what you need to pay attention to and where you should be asking questions to get the story.

For example, a big jump in income in a year looks great but it might not be. It could be the result of a merger, or a large, restricted donation. Still sounds positive, well it might be but it could also present its own challenges, particularly if the big donation is to be spent over more than one year, because you'll have all the income in one year and the expenditure in another.

An indicator says look at me there is something going on here. If you want more detail, well that's the time to refer to the text of the accounts, as this should provide a context for these numbers.

Drawing this section to a conclusion, if income is growing, surplus is growing and assets are at least a quarter of income, then at first glance this all looks positive.

One caveat is that the numbers give you a snapshot of how healthy the organisation was at the last financial year end. That may not be how things are now, but it's a start.

People and quality

Numbers are useful in giving a quick view of what's going on in the charity but where do you get more details about the quality of the charity?

Don't trust a charity's website or social media. These belong to the charity and are the organisation's shop window. It's the place where they put all the shiniest and sparkliest stories to project the kind of charity that they are.

In conversations with the chief executive of a very large national charity, whom I was a little in awe of, I told her that I was impressed with their website and all the great things it showed. I told her that I saw her organisation as something to aspire to be like, and I may even have really gushed at this point.

She paused, then replied by thanking me, acknowledging how polished it was, the amount of money it costs, and then listed six major challenges to her organisation that were not mentioned on the website but that kept her awake at night.

Websites and social media are our best face, presenting the image we want to project of our organisation. They are us on our best day. They have their usefulness in that they give a feel for the range of work of the charity, but only in its broadest context. If the website is old-fashioned and limited in information, then that tells you something about what's going on in the charity. If the postings are out of date, or if it has a huge donation page, or if it contains the voices of the people it is here to serve, well, all of that tells you something too. They are not without worth, and are a useful place to start, but you work in the charity and have an inside track, so the best way for you to find out about what's going on in your charity is to talk honestly with the people who work in it and the people who are served by it.

Talking to people

In this initial overview I've purposefully grouped together people and quality because initially the way you will best get a feel for the quality of what the charity does is by visiting people, seeing where they work and having conversations with as many as possible.

You will need to talk to people across the organisation as no one person knows everything. Information sits in pockets around the charity.

The written information, the reports and the external views from auditors and regulators will give you so much - and will also provide a framework to measure what you are told when you talk to people. For instance, if the person you talk to tells you how wonderful their service is but the regulator has expressed concerns, and the service budgets show large expenditure on agency staff, then that's the start of a conversation.

For a depth of understanding of what's really going on, the only way is to talk to people, and not just your line reports, but the people at the sharp end.

Be humble

If you are the new kid in a charity, then you'll know less about it than nearly everyone else. If you want to know more, then get out and about and talk with the people who know more, the people with a lived experience of what the charity is like.

If you think you know your charity but haven't been to visit people in the past 12 months, then you are out of date and need to talk to people who know more about how things are now, rather than how they used to be.

This isn't about summoning people to your office. This is about going to where people are, seeing where they work and the equipment they have. If you are trying to find out what's going on, then go to their turf and get a smell of the place.

The fact that you make the effort to go and see them is of benefit, but just going there is not enough, there are some factors that will affect how successful these visits are.

Go alone

If you want people to be honest with you then they are more likely to do this one-to-one than if their line manager is also in the meeting. That's not to say that everyone has an overbearing boss, but we are more likely to be open in a one-to-one conversation than in a group of people who do not know each other very well.

Meeting people individually also means that you hear the quiet reflective people with equal weight to the more vocal minority who tend to dominate in groups.

Be aware of positional power

I'm sure you are lovely but the fact that a 'higher-up' in the charity wants to come and talk with a front-line worker can put people on edge, particularly if it's not part of the usual culture.

When I worked for Scope, the lovely Sharon Collins was Director of Services overseeing delivery across the country, for both Children and Adult Services and was responsible for a team of 2,500 people.

She explained to me that when she turned up at a service it was for one of three reasons.

1. Someone has done something really good.
2. Someone had done something really bad.
3. It was part of a routine visit, and people will have prepared for it in advance and tidied up, and maybe made sure that some members of the team were on shift and some not.

Sharon was also the first person to tell me that 'the Queen thinks that the world smells of fresh paint'.

It's natural for people to try and impress and show you the best of what they do, but it can get in the way of really understanding what is going on.

There is absolutely nothing you can do about this apart from being clear that the person you are going to see is not in trouble; that you just want to come and see for yourself; and that you want to get to know the organisation better.

Be human

You have a responsibility to be a human being when you go and visit. Remember that you are a disruption to people doing their job; they are doing you a favour; and the success of getting people to talk to you honestly will be affected dramatically by your ability to be a colleague rather than a boss - even if you are the boss.

Be helpful, offer to come and do a task. Sit on reception, shadow a colleague, get involved with 'the doing' of the organisation. You'll seem more approachable by doing something, and if you do it less well than the people who do it all the time, well that's to be expected. People will appreciate that you are trying.

Be honest

Getting out and talking with people is a great chance to get yourself known and to see what's going on in the charity. It's also a great chance to be honest with people about the position of the charity, to set the expectation when things have to change, and to start engaging people in that change. You get to show that you treat people like adults and to show some trust.

Being honest takes courage. The fear is that if you share the things that are bad and not working, your colleagues will think that the charity is going to fail, and they will leave creating another gap and another issue in the charity.

The reality is that they might. Some people will be scared of this and choose to move on, some will come on board and embrace the challenge, and some will resist every step of the way. It's always good to know who you are working with. The only way to find that out is to go and visit people and to talk with them honestly.

We can't force people to stay. We can encourage and persuade, but at the end of the day people choose who they work for. We are all volunteers, even those of us who are paid.

Avoid blame

Your charity might be in a state, and it might be easy to point fingers at those who had gone before, or those who are still around, but how does that move you on? What it will do is communicate to your colleagues that you're not above blaming and trying to foist responsibility to other people. Who wants a leader like that? Rather than blaming, focus on where you want to get to and adopt a wobbly wheels approach.

Having a shopping trolley with a wobbly wheel isn't going to stop you buying your weekly shop, but it is annoying.

Where I do my weekly shop, they used to have a system where you put a 'wobbly wheels' tag on a shopping trolley when you put it back in the rack. Then someone would come and fix them. I always thought this would happen in the dead of night when the store was closed, and no one was around. Unseen people quietly going about their work righting the things that are wrong (like superheroes but with spanners).

Fixing the wobbly wheels of a shopping trolley is a small thing, but it does remove an irritation in shopping. It also made me feel like people were paying attention and not to oversell this, they cared enough to try and sort things out.

What I like most about this though is that there's no blame here. Something is not working so they take responsibility and fix it.

If your charity has had a failure of governance, or that the senior team failed in their duty to run the organisation properly, the key point is to identify the issues and address them.

If you have a problem here and now, then as we've already established, you're it, and the only question that really matters is 'How will you sort it out?'

Ask and listen

Talking honestly to people is a great way of building trust, but it's a rubbish way of finding out what's going on. For that you need to ask questions, and most importantly listen to what they tell you. You have one mouth and two ears and that's a good ratio for talking and listening.

Remember you are trying to find out what's going on in their service, and they know more about this than you so give them the space to tell you. Ask them what works and what doesn't, ask them what makes their jobs more difficult, and ask them what you can do to help them, and then if you can solve it quickly, do. It may be the first thing that a senior person in the organisation has done for them recently or at all.

When I asked someone why a bathroom door was missing a lock, I was told that it had been like that for an age, and that they kept asking for it to be fixed but it never quite made it on to the central property team's priority list. I made a call (remember you do have positional power but be careful how you use it) and then checked back the next week to make sure it was fixed. It was a little thing, but it made a difference. It starts to show that you will do what you say, and not to oversell this, that you care enough to try and sort things out.

After your visit, send them a thank you email, tell them what you have done following the discussion. By showing that you've listened to what they have to say you'll build trust.

Move at the speed of trust

Move at the speed of trust is a great saying. I don't know who said it first, but I do know that you build trust by doing, and then by being consistent.

We build an understanding of how the world works based on our previous experiences. If the first time you encountered a dog it bit you, then the next time you encounter a dog it would not be unreasonable if you were a little wary.

If however, you have 100 positive experiences of dogs then you are likely to expect your next experience to be positive. We build trust.

It is just an expectation of how someone will behave, based on previous experience and I'm always amazed how quickly trust can be built.

Trust works in both directions. You will show that you can be trusted to do what you say, but you will also need to demonstrate trust in your colleagues, trust that they are trying to do their best and that means that occasionally you have to cut them some slack.

We all have it within us to motivate ourselves but we sometimes benefit from a bit of encouragement to do our best. There are days when I start the day with a run, work hard and finish the day feeling satisfied with a job well done, and then there are other days when the alarm goes off that all I want to do is pull the duvet over my head and go back to sleep. Those are the days that I could do with a bit of extrinsic motivation, someone to say 'Come on...'.

Obviously, you and I are complex individuals working in an ever-changing world. It's useful to pause and recognise that our colleagues are also complicated, emotional human beings just as we are.

In your charity you have a group of adults working in a community to deliver on a common purpose. They will have their individual strengths, stuff they struggle with and also their own understanding about what is important in their job.

We are all individuals, but we come together in an organisation so what is important is that we are aligned to the purpose of the charity and that we are pulling in the same direction even if we are not necessarily all following exactly the same path.

I hold on to the fact that when two people do the same thing it is not the same and that's great. We're people, not robots, and bringing the diverse skills and approaches of all of your colleagues will make you a richer organisation. (We pick this up again in the chapter 'Having a plan'.)

Equifinality is a social science term that captures this alignment but diverse approaches. Sometimes you can get the same results by following different paths in the same general direction, or as the cat skinners say, 'there is more than one way...'.

Any organisation is just a group of people trying to achieve a purpose. So set the expectations, give people the tools they need to do their jobs well, and then trust them get on with it...but please remember you have responsibility for delivering on the purpose of the charity so make sure you check in regularly to see that they are still aligned.

The truth

I like to think that people are honest.

They might be reticent to share their hopes and worries with you if their previous experience in the charity is that those who complain get dumped on, but if they share with you, they will share what they see, and what they believe to be true.

Their truth though is very different from 'The Truth'.

My favourite story about this is that in a 1990s, a radio station brought together two people connected to the Vietnam War - a journalist who was reporting on the White House and one of the generals who was there at the time.

Thirty years had passed and the journalist asked how much of what he had written at the time was correct. The general paused and then gave him his due, most of it. Then the general added a caveat, he said it was like the journalist was outside of the room peering through the keyhole.

What he could see, he reported on and reported accurately, but his field of vision was narrow. He couldn't see everything else that was going on in the room, and he couldn't hear the conversations, so he had missed the wider context. The bigger picture.

The journalist was right in what he said but it was a keyhole of truth.

Keyholes of truth

The truth that people will share with you is from their perspective. It's true and has real value, but it may not be able to take in the whole context.

One of the great things about my role is that I get to talk to lots of people and see the organisation from lots of different points of view. I see the trends (just like the finances), the repeating patterns, the concerns and the gripes that are raised time and again, and pulling all this together gives a fuller picture of what's going on and why people work for your charity.

Time

There is no shortcut to this. If you want to know what's going on in your organisation, then it's going to take time and effort. Visits need to be long, half a day at least. If you are new or you've never met the people who you are going to see, then you'll need to get over that initial formality, and that takes time. People need to be given the opportunity to get comfortable, to relax in your company and decide how much they will share with you.

In working out what we're here for, and in evaluating where you are, you'll spend time gathering information, look at the finances, read internal reports and board papers, and to really understand your organisation spending time at the sharp end.

Visits provide so much information. Sure, you'll get a feel for how engaged people are, but you'll also see the condition of the buildings that people are working and living in, the tools that people use to do their roles, including the IT they use. You'll have observed the relationships between colleagues, and the way they relate with the people that they are here to support. You'll have an idea of the terminology used on the ground and how connected the messages are on the website and financial reports to what is actually going on at the front end.

You'll have an understanding of whether the structure and processes are helping or hindering those at the sharp end, and how much trust is placed in your front-line colleagues.

From all of this information, you'll gain a wider view of what it is your charity does, how well you do it, and you'll build your own version of the truth that will be so much richer than you can ever get from just sitting in your office looking at a set of reports or dashboards.

Understanding the whole

Gestalt is a German word which loosely translates as 'whole', 'pattern' or 'form'. Gestalt is an understanding that comes not from the individual elements but only in the appreciation of the whole thing.

Oliver Sacks was a clinical neurologist and a writer. His books are wonderful and focus on the people, and how they are affected by the conditions and diseases of the brain. He writes with compassion and it's this interest in people that shines through his writing.

One of the things I love about his case studies is that they all have titles that come straight from Sherlock Homes, but instead of 'A Scandal in Belgravia' and 'The Adventure of the Creeping Man', we have 'The Island of the Colour Blind', 'The Disembodied Lady', and my particular favourite, 'The Man who Mistook his Wife for a Hat'.

The Man who Mistook his Wife for a Hat' tells the story of a professor of music who loses the ability to recognise faces and everyday items. He can describe them, and when given a glove describes it as 'a continuous surface enfolded on itself with five outpouchings', but as to what it is he can't say, though he does suggest that it could be a purse for five types of coins.

The name of the story comes from him identifying a head shaped thing as a hat. He tries to pick it up and put it on, but as he grabs it, there is a cry from his wife, and he realises that he has hold of her head.

Dr Sacks points to other people with the same condition who can only identify people if they have some outstanding detail - a big mole, or a distinctive nose, but without these markers they see only the details and are not able to form a complete picture that makes sense. Interestingly, Dr

Sacks recognises this as an impairment of the visual centre of the brain for as soon as the person spoke or cried out, they recognised them at once.

For us as we get to know the charity we will see parts of it. The challenge for us is not to see this as 'a continuous surface in-folded on itself with five outpouchings' but to see it in its entirety. Looking at parts can allow us to describe our organisation, but to understand our organisation we need to be able to put this together into a whole.

In building your understanding of the gestalt you'll need both the detail and also the width of sources, so that you don't create a keyhole of truth. This is as true for individual charities as it is for the way your charity works in a larger system, but we are getting ahead of ourselves.

> ### Questions to ask yourself
> - Do I have an understanding of my whole organisation, both the good bits and the bits that need improving?
> - What are the areas that are cause for concern?
> - What do I know least about?

What now?

Once you start to understand your organisation you need to do something with this.

Share it. Share it with the senior team, share it with your board. Share it all in one go. Work out how things are and share all of the good things and all of the bad with the board. The whole kitchen sink. Don't elaborate or emphasise, and definitely don't omit any of the bad bits.

Just spell it out, and a plan for dealing with this bit by bit, focusing on the most important things first. If you need money for the changes that are ahead, you need to ask for it at the outset. Making changes in a charity can cost money, both in investing in a positive future and dealing with legacy issues. We'll talk more about this in the chapter on change.

In the coming chapters we'll be looking at how you can use this information to make your organisation more successful.

How do you define success? Well, that is for you to decide, but I'm fairly confident that it will have something to do with your purpose, something to do with people, quality and maybe sustainability.

If you've done the work from the previous chapter, you'll know what the purpose of your organisation is and so should be able to make a reasonable fist of defining success and understand your role as a leader in making your charity successful.

Questions to ask yourself

- What does success look like for our charity?
- What next step do I need to take to maximise the chance for success?
- How will we communicate this?

What next?

We've started by touching on understanding our purpose, where we want to go and a quick appraisal of where you are.

It is a start, but there's more to do and the rest of the book will help you dig a little deeper in the areas we've touched on already and then take this further with a review of how you make the transition from where your charity is, to where you want your charity to be.

Reflection

Be clear about what your purpose is.

The key role as a leader is to create an environment where your colleagues can thrive so that they can deliver on your purpose

Unless we are financially healthy we can't deliver on our purpose in the longer term.

Talk to and most importantly listen to colleagues across the organisation and they will share their keyholes of truth.

Be human.

Give people the tools, training and support to develop and grow but if you can't change the people, change the people.

References

Charity Commission, 2017. CC3 The essential trustee: what you need to know, what you need to do.

Sacks, Oliver. The Man Who Mistook His Wife for a Hat. Touchstone, 1998, pp. 8-22

Change is constant

How to manage big change and small change in your organisation

What you will find here:
- Emotional beings
- Big change and little change
- Kotter's model on managing change
- The 12 tips of managing yourself through change

Managing through change

I've learnt that I'm not good with change.

I'm good at bringing and organising change so that it delivers what it was meant to deliver, but I'm not good at dealing with change that is imposed on me. Change is difficult. I like predictability. I like to know what I'm doing and to be confident that what I'm doing achieves an outcome for the people that we are here to serve.

Throw uncertainty into this, the hassle and the extra work of change, the unpleasantness of redundancy processes and unhappy people and I'd just rather not. I'd rather build forward from a stable platform and make iterative improvements. That means I can build my skills and knowledge and those of my team as we all work in harmony. That sounds idyllic and that's what I'd prefer.

But sometimes change is just necessary. Sometimes you have a burning platform, there is an imperative to make a change and a need to make that change now.

Knowing how difficult I find change, before I embark on any change at all, I'll need to be confident that what we have planned is not just better than what is currently in place, but significantly better to take into account all of the work and the strife of getting there.

Does anyone like change?

In introducing any change, you are taking away the predictability from someone's day and moving them from the reality of what they know to something that at this moment doesn't exist.

There is a lot resting on your shoulders. Because you've taken the time to understand the gestalt you probably have a better idea about what's going on, and why what's planned is needed, than anyone else, but when you share your view of the world, how it can be, the sunny uplands of a new world, don't be surprised if the person that you're talking to just sees the loss of the known, upheaval and uncertainty. In this they are not wrong.

It's amazing that people will hold on to something even if they know it's not working. (There is a reason we have the saying 'better the devil you know'). At SJOG we couldn't afford to run the charity the way it had been run, and so we closed an office and restructured our support services including our HR team.

One of our HR professionals told me that, in restructuring the HR team, I didn't know what I was doing and that it would fail. Now the changes that we made to the charity at that time were the basis for its continued flourishing and was recognised with a national award for 'Charity Change Project of the Year', but my HR colleague wasn't entirely wrong.

She was right in that I didn't know what I was doing to her, and she did feel like we would fail her. In making this change to her daily routines, the way she paid her bills, we would change her **status** from being a working professional to being unemployed. It's not surprising that she expressed this emotionally.

We are creatures of habit. Some of this is just bandwidth in our brains. Reaching for the same cup, to put the same coffee at the same time of day takes very little thought. It's why we take the same route to work every day and shop in the same stores.

There is an economy of effort in building on what we know. Making choices requires a bit more from us and with so much going on in our lives we fall into patterns of behaviour. It's sensible and a good use of our mental resources.

There is also some neuroscience that sits behind this. Our brains are remarkable, with more brain cells than there are stars in the sky. Even the teenager who can barely grunt in your direction has a galaxy of brain cells all working away in their heads. (Honestly there's a lot going on in there even if it's not always evident!)

We have constellations in our heads that are shaped by our behaviour. Each time we make a choice we make a connection, making that choice again strengthens that connection. We make choices every day, and the sum of all of these decisions over time, build strong connections that creates our personality.

The clever people who collect data on all of us through our smart phones and computers use this principle. They monitor our choices, the decisions we make about what to click on, and even how long we look at a particular article, photo, or item, and that goes into building an understanding of what we think, what we aspire to, and what we might purchase. When you look at your phone it really is also looking back at you.

Now if you go to your cupboard and the coffee cup you use for your 11am coffee every day is not there, what then? Your predictability has been undone, a mild annoyance or panic sets in that it's not where it should be. A quick search in the kitchen doesn't turn it up so you have a walk around your house wondering where it's been left, and if it still doesn't show up, then it will niggle throughout the day, and that's just a coffee cup. Now scale up to removing someone's livelihood.

I say this not to scare you or put you off the idea of making the change that you've identified, but just to prepare you for the reactions of the people affected, because forewarned means you can better understand, better empathise, and better mitigate the impact of the changes.

We value predictability and don't like it when we are surprised by things jumping out of metaphorical doorways and shouting, 'Boo!'.

I used to support a young man with an acquired brain injury. His vision was so bad that unless you were standing within 12 inches, he couldn't see the shape of you. He had a reputation for being bad tempered and likely to hit people who came near. He was a young, strong man so these hits landed with force, but he also had his favourites who he didn't punch. Instead, he unleashed a smile at them, and it was a big, beautiful smile.

He didn't have the language to explain why, but through observation, the people who, not unreasonably, approached nervously were more likely to be hit. The people who were his favourites greeted him warmly and he responded warmly with a big, beautiful smile.

The understanding we arrived at was that from his point of view, those people who didn't greet him came out of nowhere, and his reaction to the shock was to try and push them away, which often resulted in a hit. Those who said hello gave him just enough time to know that someone was coming,

That ability to know what is coming is important to us all. That is what our routines give us; that is why we get excited with the anticipation of seeing friends, that's why we have a weekly shop, and regular national festivals that give shape to our year. We build little moments of predictability into our days so that we can deal with all the unexpected things that will happen.

In a work context, launching on a change project undermines that predictability, and no matter how sure you are that the change will be for the better and excited for the change, your colleagues may not feel the same way.

We are emotional beings and that need for predictability has to be addressed, or it will come out as resistance, a refusal to engage, or the sharing of their opinion that it will never work.

You can help this by thinking through the process before you start, putting in appropriate support for those affected and building as much predictability into the process as possible.

As I said, sometimes change is inevitable and particularly when you have a burning platform that needs addressing.

Questions to ask yourself
- Why do I want to go through a change programme?
- How will it not only be better but significantly better to make it worth going through all the heartache of a change process?
- Who will be my support and sounding board?

Burning platforms and melting icebergs

The concept of burning platforms is from Kotter, who for me is the king of change management. I buy into his model wholeheartedly, but I would suggest don't go and read his book which is intuitively named 'Managing Change' but instead pick out the less obviously titled 'Our Iceberg is Melting' which is all about penguins. I love this book.

Our Iceberg is Melting is an allegory about a group of penguins. The challenge is, you've guessed it, their iceberg is melting (rather than their platform burning).

Reading it on a train will draw looks from the people around you because it is laugh out loud funny, and whilst they are penguins, you'll recognise the people that we all have in our organisation including the excellently named 'Nono the penguin' who maintains that it will never work and will look to undermine the changes because they want to hold on to what they know.

The penguins in the story follow the eight stages of Kotter's change management process in a funny and engaging way, and then backs up all of this with the serious management theory from Kotter in the second half of the book.

Kotter's 8 stage process for leading change is:

1. Create a sense of urgency
2. Build a guiding coalition
3. Form a strategic vision and initiatives
4. Enlist a volunteer army
5. Enable action by removing barriers
6. Generate short-term wins
7. Sustain acceleration
8. Institute change

But trust me, read about the penguins, it will all become clear.

Burning platforms and prioritising risk

We shared at the beginning that in 2018 we had a burning platform. We were losing £35,000 a week and we had no reserves. Demonstrable quality in the charity was patchy, and after years of the charity shrinking, the narrative in the charity was that the charity was in terminal decline. Consequently, the trustees had sensibly decided that if the charity couldn't be turned around in 12 months, then it would close.

Even if you come into the charity knowing this there are always surprises.

In the initial stages it felt like every stone we turned over had a monster under it. Some of these represented a legal, compliance or safety risk and were dealt with immediately. Some rocks though, had poor practice, or potential future implications under them and we had to choose and turn back over the stone, resolving to deal with that particular monster later.

It's uncomfortable and not a situation that anyone would want to be in, but there are only so many resources in the charity, and so you have to prioritise and carry a degree of risk.

We all have our own comfort levels around risk. Some have an appetite for risk, others are risk adverse, but regardless, there is a level of risk that you will need to carry. Most important is that ability to identify which is an immediate risk and which can wait.

Significant risks should be on the organisation's risk register, which the trustees have ownership of. They are ultimately accountable and so you need to keep them informed.

An often-overlooked factor in managing change is managing yourself through the change process. You are an emotional being and if you are going to see your way through this you will need to take care of yourself.

The 12 tips of managing yourself through change

Like most people I love predictability, with a soupcon of variability. When I go to the supermarket, I have a core shopping list in my head, the things I buy every week, but then I'll throw in a few different things, just for a change, and to keep my mealtimes varied.

If the shop had none of my regular items I'd be thrown. My understanding of how my weekly shopping should be done would lose all its core predictability, and I may become a little annoyed, upset or even choose to shop elsewhere.

So, if you are going to embark on a programme that is going to upset your colleagues' sense of predictability, expect a response. Be strong, because you will need a barrel load of resolve to get through this, and here are 12 tips to help you get through this.

1. **Be clear about why you are doing this.**

    No charity has a right to exist. Sometimes it's easier just to let organisations fail or close them down. Change programmes are hard, and if you are not up for months of work, and people telling you that you are wrong, then walk away now.

    If you are going to get involved with a change programme, then when times are darkest, understanding the purpose and being clear about 'the why' you embarked on this in the first place is really important. Make sure this is written down and shared widely.

2. **Make sure that you have the board agreement.**

    Provide them with a 'warts and all' assessment of the situation. Don't try and protect them from the full scale of the situation. Legally, they are responsible and they need to know.

3. **Include the kitchen sink.**

    In providing the board with information tell them all the bad news at once. Don't keep coming back with more bad news at each board meeting. Roll it all up into a big ball and deliver it in one go. If you need time to identify all of the bad stuff, then take the time to do this properly, but do it quickly.

4. **Have a plan.**

    Provide all the bad news to the board in one go, but have options for how you would like to address this, and make sure it's costed. If you are asking for money, build in a contingency, ask for it all in one go and then stick to this.

5. **Share the plan.**
   Talk to everyone in the organisation as often as possible. Talk to them honestly about the current situation, the reason that change is necessary, the measures that have been identified and ask for their help in finding new measures. If the plan changes, share that too and the 'why' behind the change of direction.

6. **Talk to people.**
   Communicate regularly even if there is nothing to say about the changes. Talk about the visits that you've had, the pieces of work that have been completed. Sometimes what you say is less important than the fact that you are willing to demonstrate that you value and respect your colleagues enough to share stuff with them.

   I have teenagers. Some of the things that they share with me have worth, not because I'm particularly interested in the subject, but because they are choosing to share a little bit of what is important to them. Your colleagues will value you sharing a little bit of what is important to you. Be human. Bring your whole self to work.

7. **Just because it's not personal, doesn't mean it's not personal.**
   This work is sometimes unpleasant. Redundancies should never be personal, but it will feel personal to the people you are making redundant. You are taking away the means of supporting themselves and their family and introducing uncertainty into their lives. If you are new to the charity, then you'll seem to have strolled in and decided that they are not needed in the organisation when they have put so much more into it than you have.

   You are telling them that they are not a vital part of the charity that they belong to, and that's tough for anyone to hear. So, if you are making redundancies be human about it, and as all human beings are emotional creatures expect people to respond emotionally.

8. **This is a team sport.**
   You will have people telling you that it can't be done, or that you are going against the values of the organisation, or that it won't work.

They're being honest with you. They believe it and it is true from their point of view. They might not have a full understanding of your plan, indeed they may only have glimpses (Keyholes of Truth), but it's all valid feedback, so take this and evaluate it but balance it with other views and voices.

Have an ally within the organisation, or a mentor or friend who can offer an alternative view, or if you can build a team that can help share the load, and who you can turn to and say, 'well what do you think', then so much the better.

9. **It takes time.**
Pace yourself for the long haul and give yourself a break if things take longer than you expect. The initial turnaround at SJOG took 12 months. This was fast, but that was because we only had 12 months to save the charity.

We've always made progress, but the path has been more like a meandering river than an arrow. The direction has always been towards the sea but not always directly towards the sea.

We dealt with the big monsters, the things that could break the charity, but two and half years later we just about came to the end of dealing with last of the 'legacy' monsters.

10. **Good people will choose to leave.**
We are all volunteers. We trade our labour to a cause that we believe in, even if that is only because it pays our bills. As individuals, we can choose to shift allegiance to another organisation that we think can better deliver on what we are hoping to achieve or has better benefits.

Whether driven by cause, better pay or a kinder work environment, people will choose to leave you, and during periods of change that rate of people moving on is likely to increase. It does get easier though.

11. **It will get easier.**
But it will take time. If you are moving from one situation to another then you will have those people who will get behind the new plan

quickly, the early adopters, then you will have the mass of people who will come on board, and finally you will have a tail who will get on board only right at the very end.

Previously, I worked on bringing two charities together into a new entity. I was one of the first members of staff of the new organisation, and when I met people, they would introduce themselves as 'Hi I'm Bob I'm from Charity A', or 'Hi, I'm Jaspreet and I come from Charity B'.

Whenever I heard this, I would challenge it and remind them they worked for the new entity now.

It started to niggle more and more and then, some months later I was in a meeting with colleagues when someone started to talk about taking a certain approach because they were from Charity A. I paused, let the comment sit and then one of his colleagues who had worked in the same organisation challenged him, told him that he was part of a new organisation, and that he was out of step with the rest of the charity. He went a step further and said that he should get on board or choose to move on. I knew at that point we were 'over the hump' and I never had to mention it again.

It's tough in those early stages. You might feel like you are the only one banging the drum, but it's a gradual transition and with constant repetition and time, we get there. Resistance wanes over time, as people can see not just what you are promising for the future, but that the things you said would happen did happen. Eventually, there is a point where the people who dig their heels in and refuse to get on board either move on or become the outliers in your organisation.

12. **Look for the wins and celebrate them.**
There are totemic moments on the path of change. These need to be marked and sensitively celebrated. The changes in SJOG had a number of totemic moments:

- The change of branding was telling everyone in the charity that we had changed, and that the way we spoke about ourselves was more positive

- The spending of money on bringing people together when we were making losses was a decision that I thought about twice, but bringing people together to talk about successes in the charity was the right thing to do. In a workshop session listening to our colleagues talk, I realised that there had been a change in the organisation and an understanding about what we were building towards

- The posting of the first monthly surplus was big, though one swallow does not a summer make. Following it up with two more months for an increasingly successful quarter was more cause for celebration

- The biggie was posting a surplus at the end of the first year and presenting the board with the following year's budget with a healthy and entirely achievable surplus. It made me feel like we had steadied the ship. Not that the job was done and we'd reached the end, but that we'd reached the end of the beginning. There's always more to do, but we had turned the ship round in 12 months, and were at the end of the initial change process

These little wins and celebrations are markers on the path. They help to build confidence and they take the edge off any imposter syndrome, but we'll cover more in the chapter on Managing Yourself.

Big change, little change

I said at the beginning that I'd much rather not go through big changes. I like incremental changes that build one little improvement on another. I like the idea of taking a step and then another step, so that by improving 1% and another 1% we get to where we want to get to through a process of evolution rather than revolution. Less emotion and more predictability.

If you don't have a burning platform and are happy to take your time then I urge you to go for this approach, but the 12 tips still apply.

You'll still need to know where you are going, have a plan of how to get there, involve the team and celebrate the wins, but there's less drama with evolution than revolution.

The only other thing to remember is that change is constant. We continue to strive to be better at what we do, and make sure that our organisation can better deliver on its purpose. Change is what we do.

Questions to ask yourself

- Are you clear about the change you are trying to achieve?
- Are you clear that change processes are hard, and they are extra work on top of what your organisation does?
- Are you clear about where your help and resolve will come from?

Reflection

- Change is constant.
- Change programmes work best when you are clear about what you are trying to achieve.
- Change processes are hard and they are extra work on top of what the organisation already does.
- There will be things that are difficult, and these will need resolve and support to get through.

References

Kotter, John, and Holger Rathgeber. (2017) Our Iceberg is Melting. Macmillan

Assurance

The role of governance in keeping your organisation from falling over

What you will find here:

- Understanding governance, why it is important and where it fits in your charity
- Building a governance structure that delivers
- Developing a board

Why focus on governance?

I expect for many people, this is the last chapter you may have turned to in this book. Governance is sometimes seen as the dry subject, the boring bit, the part that adds least value, the necessary evil, and is often neglected in favour of day-to-day operational matters, growth and exploring new initiatives.

In reality, it couldn't be more important in adding value to a charity. Good governance is likely to lead to a more effective, sustainable organisation, delivering on its purpose and achieving outcomes.

Apart from the regulatory and compliance matters (more later!), good governance ensures the organisation stays true to, and delivers on, its purpose and guides the charity to long term success, whatever the size or scale.

Delivering benefit

Charities exist to improve the world for the beneficiaries that they support and to do this both today and into the future. The responsibility for ensuring that charities deliver public benefit sits with the charities' trustees.

In Guidance CC3a, the Charity Commission also requires charity trustees to exercise prudence and 'not take inappropriate risks with the charity's assets or reputation'. Indeed, trustees can be personally and corporately responsible if they fail to exercise prudence in their governance.

So, charity trustees must change the world, but in a responsible manner, ensuring they are fulfilling their fiduciary responsibilities. To help them in this, organisations such as the NCVO (National Council of Voluntary

Organisations) and ACEVO (Association of Chief Executives of Voluntary Organisations) have come together to create The Good Governance Code for Voluntary Organisations. This is supported by the Charity Commission.

In meeting the guidance contained in the good governance guide, trustees will ensure that their organisation remains legal and is protected from financial and reputational damage. However, a compliance agenda of this sort will not ensure that a charity is successful or competitive.

This is the challenge for trustees. Governance is a hygiene factor, the plumbing of the organisation. It goes on working in the background and is only noticed when it doesn't work.

Reputation

Charities do good in society; they exist for public benefit and historically enjoy a strong reputation.

Primarily what affects an organisation's reputation is not just its ability to be of benefit, but to be seen to be doing good. Building credibility and perceived success in delivering social change can build an organisation's profile, through increased profile can come increased funding (who is going to fund an organisation they've never heard of?) and through increased funding comes the opportunity to do more, and to be seen to do more good.

What is governance?

The Cadbury Commission Report in 1992 defined governance as follows:

> "Corporate governance is the system by which companies are directed and controlled. Boards of directors are responsible for the governance of their companies."

This is a definition relating to the corporate world and whilst the principles of accountability are transferrable to charities, there is not the same shareholder relationship in not-for-profit organisations.

Cornforth (2003) helpfully defines governance specific to voluntary organisations as:

"The systems and processes concerned with the overall direction, effectiveness, supervision and accountability of an organisation."

This definition feels more appropriate to charities and makes governance seem more relevant and less overwhelming to tackle, especially for smaller organisations.

In Charity Law and Governance: A Practical Guide (2018), the four aspects above are explained as:

- **Direction:** providing leadership, setting strategy and being clear about what the organisation is aiming to achieve and how it is going to do it.

- **Effectiveness:** making good use of financial and other resources to achieve the desired outcomes.

- **Supervision:** establishing and overseeing controls and risk management, and monitoring performance to make sure that the organisation is on track to achieve its goals, making adjustments where necessary and learning from mistakes.

- **Accountability:** reporting to those who have an interest in what the organisation is doing and how it is doing it.

In recent years, the Charity Commission has done much work to help charities understand and improve their governance. A succession of high-profile charities failing due to ineffective governance has brought this even more to the fore.

The Charity Governance Code, a follow on from Good Governance: A Code for the Voluntary and Community Sector (June 2005), sets out seven key principles, supported by statements of recommended practice, which aims to set out a clear framework on governance, for organisations to follow. It is not a legal or regulatory requirement but aims to help charities and boards develop high standards of governance.

The charity governance code

The seven key principles were refreshed in 2020 and are as follows:

1. **Organisational purpose:** The board is clear about the charity's aims and ensures that these are being delivered effectively and sustainably.

2. **Leadership:** Every charity is led by an effective board that provides strategic leadership in line with the charity's aims and values.

3. **Integrity:** The board acts with integrity. It adopts values, applies ethical principles to decisions and creates a welcoming and supportive culture that helps achieve the charity's purposes. The board is aware of the significance of the public's confidence and trust in charities. It reflects the charity's ethics and values in everything it does. Trustees undertake their duties with this in mind.

4. **Decision-making, risk and control:** The board makes sure that its decision-making processes are informed, rigorous and timely, and that effective delegation, control and risk assessment and management systems are set up and monitored.

5. **Board effectiveness:** The board works as an effective team, using the appropriate balance of skills, experience, backgrounds and knowledge to make informed decisions.

6. **Equality, diversity and inclusion:** The board has a clear, agreed and effective approach to supporting equality, diversity and inclusion throughout the organisation and in its own practice. This approach supports good governance and the delivery of the organisation's charitable purposes.

7. **Openness and accountability:** The board leads the organisation in being transparent and accountable. The charity is open in its work, unless there is good reason for it not to be.

Fig 4. The key elements of the Charity Governance Code

Helpfully, the code also sets out clear rationale for each principle, the key outcomes from successful delivery on the principle, and a checklist of recommended best practice for each of larger and smaller charities.

Whether tackling governance for the first time or health checking and overhauling existing governance structures, this code could not be more helpful. At SJOG we took one principle at a time, reviewed the recommended practice, identified the gaps or shortcomings in our processes and created an action plan to address them. It is not something that can be achieved overnight but the clear structure is manageable. It is important to remember that these are stretch targets in terms of governance standard. Moving in the direction towards achieving them is what is most important.

The importance of the board

Going back only a couple of years, the SJOG board was made up almost entirely of older white men, predominantly Brothers from the Order that had started the charity in the UK many years ago.

Every person on the board had the best interests of the charity at heart and was committed to its longevity and delivering on our purpose, of that there is no doubt. However, I think it is also fair to say that the board lacked diversity and a full understanding of the charity code. Over the next two years, the board was revitalised through development of the current trustees, recruitment of new trustees, clear terms of reference, effective meeting agendas and good use of committees.

Boards change over time. The current board will continue to develop but it is now a more diverse and informed group with varied skills and backgrounds working collectively to make decisions that set the direction of the charity and our progress towards it.

What does a board do?

A board of trustees has overall responsibility for the governance of the charity. It has compliance and regulatory responsibilities and also has a supporting and monitoring role.

In the case of many charities, like SJOG, that are charities and companies limited by guarantee, the trustees are also company directors and hold all the legal responsibilities that come with that position. Your charity may have different names for its trustees, they may be governors, directors, executive committee, or some other name. What is important is the role and that the members understand the extent of their role on the board.

NCVO sets out the following as the main responsibilities of the charity board:

- Furthering the charity's overall purpose, as set out in its governing document, and setting its direction and strategy - for example, by developing plans and strategies and monitoring progress

- Ensuring the work of the charity is effective, responsible and legal - for example, by the use of policies and procedures and systems for monitoring and evaluating the charity's work

- Safeguarding finances, resources and property and ensuring they are used to further the charity's purposes for example, by insuring and documenting assets, maintaining financial systems, monitoring income and expenditure and ensuring the charity is financially sustainable or viable

- Being 'accountable' to those with an interest or stake in or who regulate the charity - for example, by preparing annual reports and accounts and consulting with stakeholders

- Being clear about the people who carry out work on behalf of the charity - trustees, staff, volunteers - establishing and respecting boundaries between the governance role of the board and operational or day to day matters

- Ensuring the board operates effectively, for example, ensuring it receives the right reports and advice, by planning the recruitment and induction of trustees, providing trustees with support and training or carrying out reviews or appraisals of the board's effectiveness

Most board work will be carried out at meetings, monthly or quarterly, where the management team should provide sufficient information to facilitate discussion and quality decision-making. There may be sub-committees where work is done and decisions are delegated.

We have sub-committees for Finance & Risk and Quality, but these may not be needed in a smaller organisation where everything can be dealt with at board. The level of detail and the extent to which trustees are involved will usually depend on the size and complexity of your charity.

It is important though, to maintain the clear distinction between governance and management and a brief yet clear Terms of Reference will help with this. An example template is included at the end of this chapter (page 82, figure 4a).

Questions to ask yourself

- Do we have a diverse board with a broad range of skills, experience and background?
- Does the board clearly understand its role and responsibilities?
- Does the board receive enough quality information to make decisions?

Board assessment, recruitment, induction and development

To understand where knowledge or experience gaps may exist amongst your trustees, it is useful to carry out a board evaluation exercise. The Institute of Directors has a useful model for this and it will help to identify skills or knowledge gaps which the board believes are useful to fill. Then you can decide whether these gaps are best remedied through development or the recruitment of additional trustees.

If recruitment is the desired option, then it is important that this process is clear in its aims in attracting the right candidates. Think about where you advertise vacancies and how you present them as opportunities; use the recruitment process to exchange knowledge both ways. Be open about what you expect from your trustees in terms of time commitment and test their ability to fill the skills gaps you have. Do they display the values of the charity? Do they have a clear interest in what the charity does? This is a purely voluntary role so candidates need to show strong connection and interest and commitment to serve as trustees.

To ensure an effective and cohesive board, it is critical that successful members go through a thorough induction process. To be effective and successful in their role they need to have a clear understanding of the charity, its values and purpose, what it does, who it operates, where the opportunities and risks lie. Whilst they will learn a great deal from early board meetings, the more knowledge they can gain from induction, the sooner they will become effective trustees who are able to support, challenge and make decisions. At SJOG, trustees have meetings with the senior team, attend a first board meeting as an observer, are provided with an introduction to SJOG booklets, our articles of association and The Essential Guide to Being a Trustee document, and crucially, they visit at least one of our services to gain first hand experience of what we do.

Regular board development days are valuable in updating the board on changes in the charity or the environment in which it operates. They can also be used as training refreshers on governance and board responsibilities. Identifying and meeting ongoing training needs for trustees is key to maintaining board effectiveness and encouraging them to be involved in any charity events or fundraisers is a great way to keep them engaged and feel involved in the charity. Include them in any 'all staff' communications and don't be afraid to use emails in between formal meetings to keep trustees up to date. Three months between board meetings can seem a long time, especially for newer trustees.

Fig 4a. Terms of Reference Template

SJOG	Terms of Reference - Template	
Accountability and Purpose:	Core Membership List:	
	Quorum:	
Aims & Objectives:	Standing Agenda:	
Meeting Regulations:	Meeting Frequency/Duration:	
	Review:	

Reflection

- The board is responsible for assuring that the charity delivers on its purpose.
- The trustees board requires ongoing investment.

References

Cadbury, A.,1992. Report of the Committee on the Financial Aspects of Corporate Governance. London: Gee. Charity Commission, 2017.CCJ

The essential trustee: what you need to know, what you need to do. HMSO. London Cornforth, C., 2003. The governance of public and non-profit organisations. London: Routledge, p.103.

Acevo, 2020. The Charity Good Governance Code. London

Having a plan

Strategy and how to make sure that it makes a difference

What you will find here:

- A pragmatic definition of a strategy for charities
- The importance of hearing the voices of the people you support and colleagues in developing your strategy
- How to keep a strategy live and not just something on a piece of paper

Introduction

There is a lot of bunkum written about strategy.

At its simplest a strategy is a plan to get you from where you are now to where you want to be in the future. To do that you need to know where you are and where you want to get to.

We'll describe an approach to developing a strategy, discuss the importance of purpose, and we'll use the example of SJOG's strategy, 'We're here to help' to help guide you through the process.

Start with purpose?

Purpose is everything. As we discussed in the first chapter, your organisation exists to be of public benefit. The form that this takes will be contained within the governing documents for your charity.

The point of the strategy is to maximise the chance of success in delivering on your organisational purpose. It sets the direction, and it will inform the business plans that are produced to focus both your efforts and your resources.

Your strategy is a promise. It sets out what the charity will do, and as everybody in the charity will need to be clear on what the charity is doing, it should be shared and should be simple enough for everyone to understand.

Developing a strategy

When you sit down to write a strategy you are trying to work out how the world will be in three years, five years or maybe even ten years' time.

Joe Strummer said that the future is unwritten, but that's precisely what you are trying to do, to sit down with a blank piece of paper and write the future, which can be a bit disconcerting, but don't worry. We're here to help.

You can take comfort from William Goldman, the writer behind the Oscar winning 'All the Presidents Men' and 'Butch Cassidy and the Sundance Kid' as he said that,

> "Nobody knows anything... Not one person in the entire motion picture field knows for a certainty what's going to work. Every time out it's a guess and, if you are lucky, an educated one."

So, relax. Your strategy is your best guess as to what the future holds for your organisation. You will need to write down that best guess though, share it with everyone and hope you are right and then in a few years' time be measured against this.

Still worried? Don't be.

In 2021, RSM undertook a review of 40 charities strategies from across the UK, and produced a report called 'What does a good strategy look like for charities?'. The charities used in the sample came from across the sector, from those with an income of less that £5million to large charities with an income of over £25million. They looked at what the charities promised in their strategies, how well they measured their progress, and how well they delivered on their promises

And what did they find? They found that 25% of all aims set over a five-year period were not reported on in subsequent years, and that just over 50% of aims were reported as achieved across all charities. This means that just under 50% were not reported as achieved - and if you had achieved them why wouldn't you report on them?

In summary, RSM said that, "setting, monitoring and reporting on strategic objectives is not easy," and the great thing is that everyone knows that plotting the future is an imperfect science. We make predictions, and then we work hard to make them happen, a bit like Edison inventing the future.

The strategy is a plan for how we will shape our organisation so that it has the best possible chance of delivering on its purpose.

In putting together your best guess, there is a real benefit in developing the strategy with the people who use your charity, and with your colleagues, both paid and volunteers. The benefits are three-fold:

1. The strategy is better aligned to the needs of the people that you are supporting, because you are asking them what they want from your charity rather than assuming that you know

2. Your colleagues, the people at the sharp end, will tell you the challenges they face and how they can be better supported to deliver on the purpose of the charity

3. That once the strategy is developed it is not imposed but is a collective piece of work by a community with a common purpose. That gives a mandate for the strategy

But the views of your stakeholders only deliver part of the picture.

We said that a strategy is a plan on how to get from where you are to where you want to be, and so you need to understand where you are, by undertaking a thorough review of the finances, the governance arrangements, the people, and current legislative and regulatory frameworks that you currently work within.

The world will also continue to turn, and whilst you are planning for the progress of the charity, the world will change as well. Fortunately, you are not the only one looking at this, and a whole other set of people are looking at what the changes in the world will mean for their organisations.

Governments try to predict the future. They use forecasting for the economy, for population, for the changing demographics within populations. They use this to determine how much they should invest in healthcare, where and how they develop infrastructure and the policies that they will use to nudge the behaviour of their populations. The great thing for you is that these policies are freely available, and there will also be think tanks offering their views on these policies. Read them and use them to educate your best guesses.

> **Questions to ask yourself**
> - Who are your stakeholders?
> - External to your charity, what do you need to consider, for example, what are your funder priorities and what is government policy in your area of work?

Do we really need a strategy?

You could be brave and decide that you won't develop a strategy; that your charity will just carry on doing what it does and respond to opportunities and challenges as they present themselves.

It would be one way to go, and you'd find support in R. Martin's paper for the Harvard Business Review whose title wears its heart on its sleeve. 'The big lie of strategic planning' argues that strategic plans are there to support the insecurities of chief executives rather than for the benefit of the organisation. Effectively they act like a streetlight to a drunk man, more for support than illumination.

The thing to remember is that this is not your strategy. It belongs to the trustees who are responsible for setting the direction of the charity, and then assuring that the strategy is being delivered.

The challenge for charities is that trustees have a duty in law to act prudently, ensuring that their charity is of benefit and using its resources to maximise benefit to its constituency. These resources include the people employed in the charity, the reserves that the charity holds and the daily income and expenditure. It's not just enough to say 'of course we do this', you must report on this and show your working.

All of this needs to be reported each year in the Trustees Annual Report which along with the Financial Accounts form a statutory duty for the trustees.

Without a plan, without measurement of the plan, and a view of what the future holds the trustees cannot meet this statutory duty.

So, is there another way?

You need a strategy! You need a way forward that encompasses the vision for the charity, that is prudent, yet ambitious, that contains promises to your beneficiaries, that is measurable so that you can report on progress, and that sets strategic rather than tactical goals.

What is the difference between strategy and tactics? Well, strategy is the 'What' tactics are the 'How'.

A strategic goal would be the 'What do we want to achieve?' e.g. 'We will become an attractive employer' and the tactic is the 'How we will achieve this?' e.g. 'We will pay in the top quartile for our sector'.

By setting strategic goals rather than tactical goals you will provide a degree of flexibility in the way that you shape your charity in the future. The strategic goal will remain, but as the world turns the means of delivering on that strategic goal can change.

There is a theoretical basis for this; Henry Mintzberg talks of emergent strategy. Now we could explain this further, but Karl Moore did it best in 2011 when he said:

> "Emergent strategy is the view that strategy emerges over time as intentions collide with, and accommodate, a changing reality."

Effectively an organisation learns what works and then adapts to develop a way of being that may not have been expressly intended at the outset. This approach allows the charity to respond to changes in environment including the opportunities that are presented and created.

So, there is a little wriggle room in a good strategy and there is comfort in that.

Developing a strategy - The SJOG Way

A strategy should not exist as a stand-alone document but as part of a process that states the strategic goals of the charity, supports them with a business plan that sets out the tactics of delivering on these and the measures that will be put in place to measure progress and shows how all of this is in service to the organisational purpose.

We love a good diagram at SJOG, and the following helps to sum up the approach taken in ensuring that we not only know what we are trying to achieve, but also how we will measure our progress towards this. We call this the SJOG way.

Fig 5. The SJOG Way

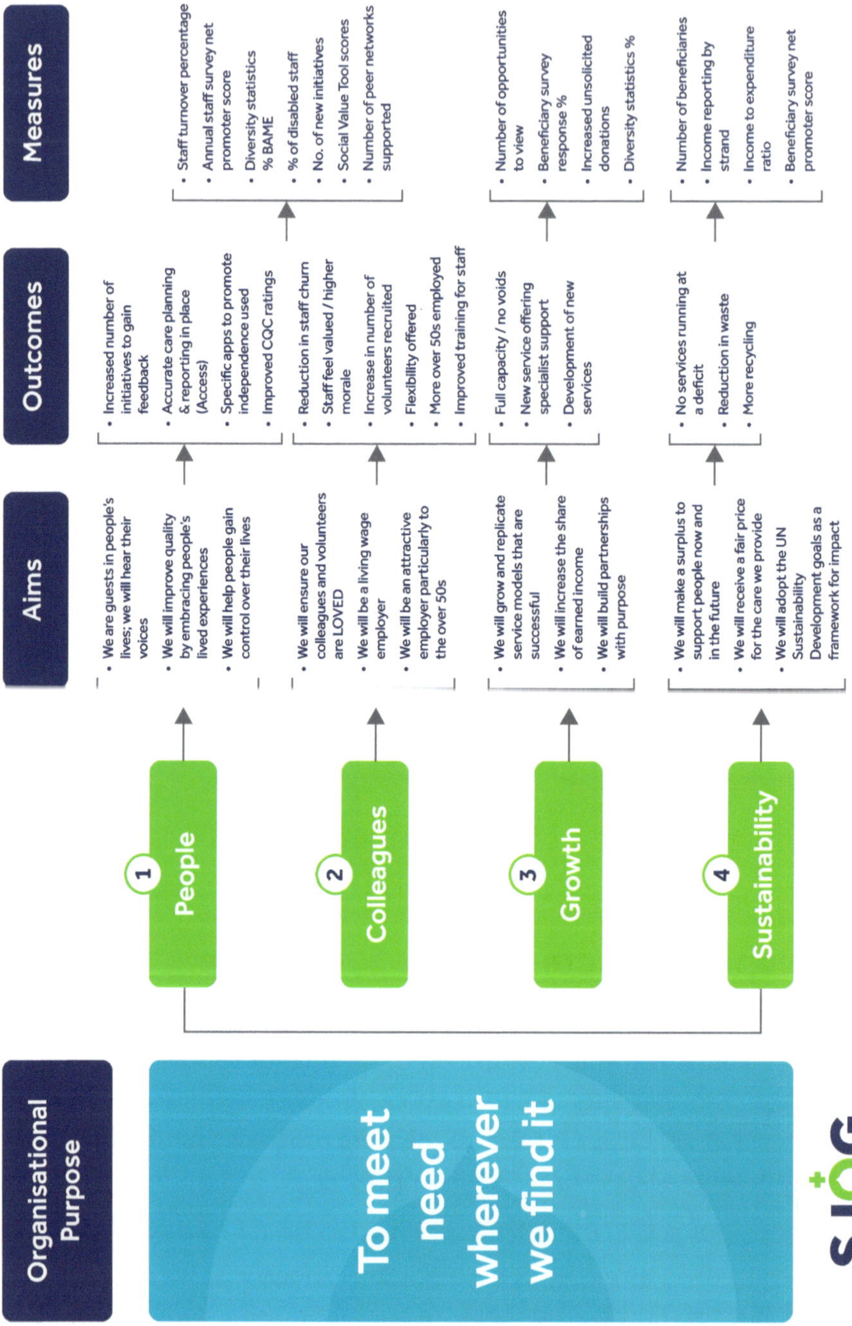
Organisational Purpose
To meet need wherever we find it
SJOG
1 People
2 Colleagues
3 Growth
4 Sustainability
Aims
Outcomes
Measures
We are guests in people's lives; we will hear their voices
We will improve quality by embracing people's lived experiences
We will help people gain control over their lives
Increased number of initiatives to gain feedback
Accurate care planning & reporting in place (Access)
Specific apps to promote independence used
Improved CQC ratings
We will ensure our colleagues and volunteers are LOVED
We will be a living wage employer
We will be an attractive employer particularly to the over 50s
Reduction in staff churn
Staff feel valued / higher morale
Increase in number of volunteers recruited
Flexibility offered
More over 50s employed
Improved training for staff
Staff turnover percentage
Annual staff survey net promoter score
Diversity statistics % BAME
% of disabled staff
No. of new initiatives
Social Value Tool scores
Number of peer networks supported
We will grow and replicate service models that are successful
We will increase the share of earned income
We will build partnerships with purpose
Full capacity / no voids
New service offering specialist support
Development of new services
Number of opportunities to view
Beneficiary survey response %
Increased unsolicited donations
Diversity statistics %
We will make a surplus to support people now and in the future
We will receive a fair price for the care we provide
We will adopt the UN Sustainability Development goals as a framework for impact
No services running at a deficit
Reduction in waste
More recycling
Number of beneficiaries
Income reporting by strand
Income to expenditure ratio
Beneficiary survey net promoter score

The approach builds on models that are widely available in the charity sector, but we've adopted and adapted it. In developing the SJOG way, and the strategic aims of the charity, we engaged our colleagues and the people that we are here to serve, and that's pivotal to the way we do things around here.

Engaging people

In order to capture the thoughts, feelings and experiences of people who are most important to the charity, there needs to be an investment of time and resources. Ideally this would be face to face conversations, but there are different ways to do this. Online surveys are useful in capturing a snapshot of opinion and can help reach large groups of people. Structured conversations, either face-to-face or virtually, enable meaningful discussion, clarification and identification of key areas of work.

The investment of time and resources is not just in the meetings, but in the preparation and the post meeting consolidation, coding and reporting of the information generated.

Our experience was that broad questions such as 'So, what should we do for the next 5 years?' are really tricky to answer.

The most fruitful discussions held were framed around the individual and what is important to them. The questions do not need to be difficult to be of use.

A life worthwhile

In 2019 SJOG embarked on developing a new strategy to refocus the charity's activities.

The prior years had seen a lack of focus with the fall out being a fall in demonstrable quality in services, lack of development of colleagues, and poor financial health.

There was a need for the charity to re-engage with its purpose, but we needed to clarify what the purpose was and how to express this simply.

Technically, the purpose of the charity is:

> "The relief of poverty, sickness, old age, distress and disabled persons."

In discussions this became expressed as:

"We're here to meet need where we find it."

We delved a bit deeper and asked what does 'meeting need mean'? By flipping the question we arrived at the simple question:

"What makes your life worthwhile?"

So in determining the strategy of the charity we asked not about the charity, but about the individual. By aggregating the results from the 112 people who took part in the process we could identify key themes that are important for people we support, our colleagues and volunteers.

Each person was asked to draw a picture of themselves and then add six arrows. At the end of each arrow they were asked to write something that made their life worthwhile (see figure 1).

Where individuals needed support, this was given to allow them to complete the task and ensure it was inclusive for all. There are no marks for artistic merit!

Fig 6. Examples of the drawings completed during the consultation

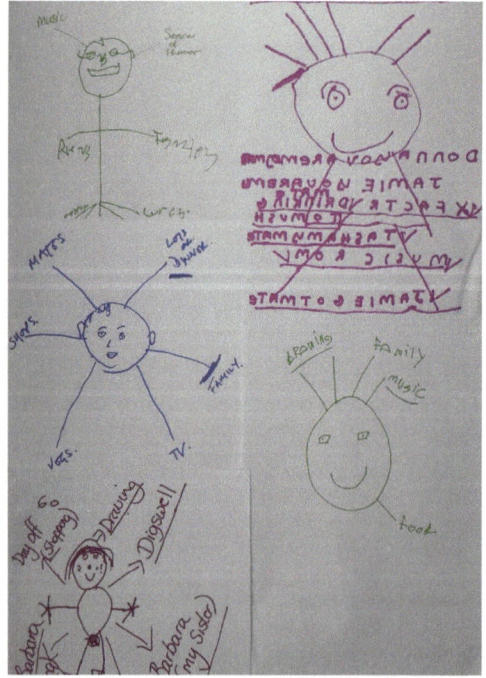

Each drawing and notes from the focus groups were analysed and responses were grouped, which led to finding the three core factors that made a life worthwhile.

These were:

- **Relationships** (having someone who is important to you, and having someone to whom you are important)
- **Purpose** (through meaningful activities) and
- **Being well** (physical and mental health)

Within these three core areas are subcategories that represented individual variations across leisure activities, faith and environment. This set our focus of how we supported the people we are here to serve.

In order to add some detail, we mapped these elements to the social determinants of health, the non-medical factors that the world health organisation recognise as influencing health outcomes.

By doing so we were able to relate the insights from to the broader external landscape of policy and research, and validate the results (see figure 7).

Fig 7. SJOG's A life worthwhile

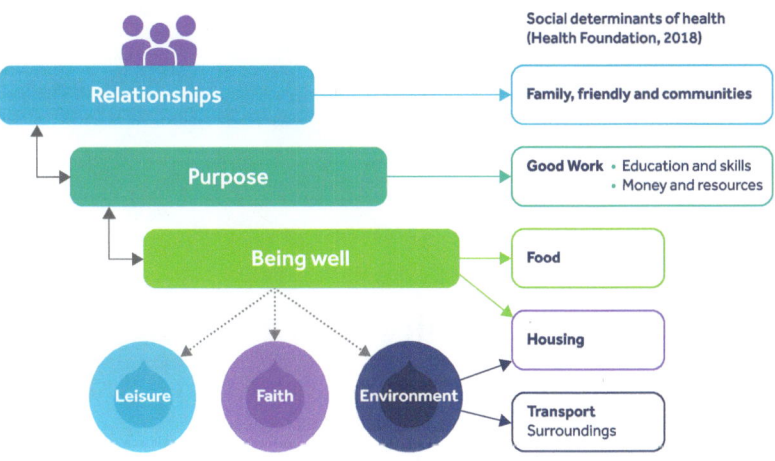

Our colleagues were involved in the process. As well as talking about the challenges they had faced and the concerns they had about an uncertain future, they also expressed their commitment stating 'We're Here to Help'.

Our colleagues' wishes for the future are the same as the people that we are here to serve. They want to be well, and SJOG supports good health outcomes for all of our colleagues through a range of initiatives. They want to be supported to deliver on their purpose, to be valued for the good work that they do, and they want to have meaningful relationships at work and a sense of belonging to something more.

Make it simple

There must be a law somewhere that says that every book must contain at least one Einstein quote (or at least a quote attributed to Einstein) and this one is no different.

It is said that Einstein stated that the answer to every problem should be as simple as possible, but no simpler. Bill Clinton's first presidential campaign summed this up with the simple acronym KISS (Keep it simple, stupid!).

There's a lot of thought that goes into a strategy, a lot of information that is generated, policies read, and considerations given to financial management, quality, and management of risk that help to provide a robust rationale for the choices in the strategy. This is helpful in reassuring trustees and demonstrating that you have put real effort into your best guess, so that it's an educated guess, but when you communicate this to your colleagues and your external stakeholders, do they really need to know that you looked at the government's population projections for the next 10 years, or do they just need to understand the direction that the charity is going in and that there is a good plan for what comes next?

Growth and sustainability

At the time of developing the 'We're Here to Help' strategy we identified that SJOG had shown little growth and that sustainability was an issue.

In terms of financial sustainability rather than stating that we would ensure £xx pounds for every service (which would be a tactical goal) we said that we would have a fair rate for the care we provide (which is a strategic goal).

We identified that the services that we had were right for now, but that the world would continue to turn and that we need to call on skills to develop alternative business models that would deliver an increased reach in the communities in which we work, and then replicate these models.

We also identified that whilst charities are classed as not-for-profit organisations, they also have to be not-for-loss to be of use in the long term, and so both existing and new services would need to be sustainable in the long term.

Sustainability is much wider than just money, and rather than devising our own set of metrics we chose to work with the UN's sustainable development goals, which benefit of being an international framework to address societal challenges facing people, planet, prosperity, and partnership.

Measure it

Writing the strategy is not the end of the process (though perhaps it is the end of the beginning). The strategy offers a framework for delivery but for trustees to be able to fulfil their fiduciary duties they need to have a method for measuring progress against the strategy.

Our suggestion would be to design your metrics and key performance indicators when you create the strategy. They act as reporting tools for board reports and are really useful in communicating with funders and commissioners, showing that progress is being made and that you are not just being busy fools.

Financial reporting is key, but we've moved on from just looking at the money to determine whether a charity is well run (I can guarantee that your purpose is not 'to be financially sustainable') and as such wider measures of impact are needed.

A common tool for this purpose is the balanced scorecard - a concept developed by Kaplan and Norton in the 1990s. The balanced scorecard is a select set of strategic measures that help you understand the key strategic drivers of performance within your organisation and monitor progress against these. It is a popular management tool with a wide variety of businesses, charities and other organisations. The key components are shown in Figure 8.

Fig 8. Balanced scorecard elements

Vision and mission	Your vision and mission as the ultimate statements of why you exist and what you want to achieve. Everything below must clearly demonstrate contribution to achieving these.
Customer	The strategic objectives that will deliver results for key stakeholders and achieve the mission in the current plan.
Business process	The objectives that capture the process you need to excel at in order to deliver results.
Learning and growth	The objectives that capture the capabilities you need to invest in, in order to excel.
Financial	The objectives that will ensure you are well resourced and use these resources efficiently.
Values	How you should behave as you fulfill the objectives to deliver the mission.

The term 'dashboard' is more current than scorecard but they can be used interchangeably, as both mean a small collection of key measures that are regularly reviewed.

Kaplan and Norton comment that how you create a balanced scorecard sets it apart from other approaches. The process of creating a balanced scorecard is almost as important as the performance management tool that is the end result.

A balanced scorecard results from mapping your strategy and identifying how key objectives are linked to each other. For example, delivering results for the people you support is dependent on financial success, which in turn is dependent on your ability to fundraise, or to operate at a surplus. The balanced scorecard encourages organisations not only to measure key results but what is driving those results.

Regardless of the exact approach you use, spend time to select the measures that work best for the charity and the work that you do. If you can, use any existing measures that might have already been identified, but only if they align nicely to the new strategy.

If you don't have these then investing in the ability to report on KPIs effectively is worthwhile in the long run, and in determining your measures, KISS, a rule that we learned the hard way!

Keep it simple, stupid!

When we developed 'We're Here to Help' we said that we would adopt the UN Sustainable Development Goals (SDGs) as a means to measure the work we were doing.

The rationale was that these are an international standard and we would be able to relate our work broadly. In reality, these are a framework rather than a set of metrics, and at our stage of development devising a structure was too complicated. We did not have the sophistication to map this against the work we delivered day to day.

In hindsight, we should have spent more time mapping out how the SDGs would be used in practice before committing to them fully. Of all of our strategic promises this is the one that we had the least success with.

Rather than get stuck we developed a bespoke set of measures and indicators (such as quality of life of the people we support, based on other work by the UN) to ensure that there was improved, detailed and regular reporting to facilitate quality decision-making.

This was a good learning lesson for us and four years on our systems have now caught up with our ambition, we've returned to the UN Sustainable Development Goals and have a two-year project that will develop a better measurement system which we are hoping can then be used as a template for other organisations.

Questions to ask yourself

- What simple question(s) would help me understand the needs of the people our charity serves?
- What can we measure which help us to understand the difference we make?
- What resources do we need to answer the two questions above?

Alive and kicking

At this point you will have your strategy fully formed and a suite of KPIs that can be used to measure progress against the strategic plan.

Next comes the challenge of embedding this across the charity and making sure that everything you and your colleagues do is aligned with the strategic plan.

Share it

Once your strategy is finalised, share it!

The strategy has been created with colleagues and the people the charity supports. It should be shared with them, preferably as a draft so that you can check that what you heard was what they said. This ensures that their involvement at the start of the process wasn't tokenistic and will help with putting the emphasis in the right place.

When producing 'We're Here to Help' we talked about colleagues throughout. Once we had a draft we went back and spoke to all of our colleagues, and in talking to volunteers, they were keen that volunteers were not lumped in with colleagues but named specifically as volunteers so that they stayed at the fore. This single change influenced how we developed our support for volunteers, as distinct and targeted, over the coming years.

Once the plan is in place, refer to it regularly in updates and use it to point to progress, so that it becomes a key reference point in the charity. Repetition is important. Let me say that again. Repetition is important.

The strategy document is not just for internal use. Time and effort went into creating it - make sure that you get the maximum value from it. It can be key in presenting externally.

At SJOG our 'We're Here to Help' strategy identified that at the heart of our services are:

- **Relationships**
- **Purpose**
- **Being well**

When seeking funding for new services we pointed back to these three elements and this was used explicitly in funding applications. The new initiatives that we created might not address all three but allowed us to show to funders that we had been robust in grounding each project.

The strategy helps when speaking externally. It provides a clear narrative for audiences and helps to draw the line from what we are doing to our wider purpose, the 'why' of the charity.

The strategy is only part of the journey

Gotta love the fact that after all this there is more to do. Do you remember that we spoke about the difference between strategy and tactics, well now's the time for tactics.

Ideally you should be able to map the actions of every person in the charity to the strategic aim.

There is a famous, and most likely apocryphal story about when JFK was on a tour of NASA during the time that the Apollo missions were being planned and saw a man sweeping up. He went over and asked him what his role was, to which the man said that he was working to put a man on the moon.

It's a nice story and it does help to highlight that everything each person does should help fulfil the purpose in some way.

Communication is important. Creating a sense of belonging to something bigger is important, but to seal the deal you can't beat some business planning and budgeting. No really!

One way to do this is to ensure that business planning and budgeting activities are mapped to the strategy. By doing a plan for the year's work this can tie into the different elements of the strategy.

At SJOG we framed our strategy as 12 promises. We presented those twelve promises to each service, each department and asked them, "what are you going to do within your team to deliver on each of these promises?" Even though we presented them with a spreadsheet to complete, and cost their suggestions, it still wasn't enough to put them off. The teams responded with gusto.

The responses varied hugely, but we had grass roots enthusiasm and creativity providing suggestions that would never have come from a top down process. Managers set their own business plans (though they were challenged on the ambition and deliverability of these). Their target for the year was to deliver the plans and the budgets that support this. Their success was reviewed in the appraisal process.

In turn the managers tasked their colleagues with delivering parts of the business plan. This set their annual targets and assessed progress through the appraisal process.

Service level plans were aggregated into an organisational business plan and budget and was more ambitious, and because it was locally owned, more likely to be delivered than if the plan had been imposed in a top-down process.

This approach aligns the work of every colleague to delivering on the strategic aims and ultimately the purpose of the charity.

We captured this diagrammatically in The SJOG Way for the organisation and then asked each manager to map their business plan against this, to develop The SJOG Way for their service or department. This creates a visual link between the work that is being done and the delivery of the strategic aim. Useful for when regulators call and an easy guide to keep everything on track, and everyone's part in putting a man on the moon!

It sounds like a lot of work and it is, but the benefits, the accountability, the engagement of colleagues and the understanding of how your work makes a difference in the lives of the people that we are here to serve pays real dividends. You'll need to budget and have an annual plan anyway so why not put in a little extra effort to deliver a joined up process.

Methodical planning is like a map. It provides direction when it's easy to feel a bit lost if unexpected events happen. Having each area of the organisation plan in this way also gives each colleague ownership. It makes the strategy tangible to them. When it comes to reporting, you can then ask each function to update you on the business plan, generating the KPI reports that you set in the strategy, and these can be used to reassure funders and demonstrate the effectiveness of your charity and your strategic planning.

We said at the beginning that putting together a strategy was a best guess and that nobody knows anything, and that's true, but looking through the other end of the telescope a strategy is not a best guess of what will happen, but a means of determining your future and shaping it.

It's said that Edison said that the best way to predict the future is to invent it and that's what you are doing shaping your charity to invent the future that you want, so that you can deliver on the purpose of your charity.

Reflection

- A strategy is simply a plan to align all the activities in a charity to ensure that it meets its purpose. It should be relevant to all parts of the organisation from the services you run through to functions like HR and finance.

- A bottom up approach to strategy development is the best way. Spend time hearing the voices of the people you support, your colleagues and any volunteers. You might also like to include some trusted external stakeholders too. By doing this in a planned way you'll be able to identify key themes that you can turn into actions. Don't forget about the external factors. Keep abreast of changes in the political and social landscape and prepare for these as much as you can.

- To make sure the strategy is alive and kicking tie it into the business planning process. This helps each colleague understand how it is relevant to them and how they can contribute.

References

RSM, 2021. Charity strategy and impact report 2021- What does a good strategy look like? https://www.rsmuk.com/ideas-andinsights/eharity-strategy-and-impact-report

Martins, R, 2014. The big lie of strategic planning. Harvard Business Review. January 2014. Harvard. Mintzberg, H. and Waters, J.,1985. Of strategies, deliberate and emergent. Strat. Mgmt. J.,6(3), pp.257-272.

Moore, K. 2011. Porter or Mintzberg: Whose view of strategy is the most relevant today. Forbes Magazine 28/03.2011

Kaplan, R. and Norton, D. (1992) The Balanced Scorecard-Measures That Drive Performance. Harvard Business Review.

A sound basis for success

The role of finance in keeping your organisation alive

What you will find here:

- Understanding what is going on, what the problems are and how to tackle them
- Setting a finance strategy and building your team as part of the organisation
- Budgeting, accountability and future focus

"We are not a business!"

It is an uncomfortable truth for some of those who work in the charitable sector that we need to place so much importance on finance when looking at the overall health of a charity. Whilst we, as not-for-profit organisations, are delighted to talk about the good things we do, the value we provide to the communities and people we support and our vision for the future, we are decidedly less comfortable with discussing our finances. It is often seen as too corporate, too business-like and 'not charitable' to those who work in our organisations, to talk about that word- money.

The sad truth is that many charities fail every year. Charities who do good work, deliver social benefit and have strong values and purposes, will fail. Not because of what they do or how they do it, or even because it is not needed. They will fail because they run out of money.

A study by Pro Bono Economics in mid-2020, found that one in ten UK charities was facing bankruptcy by the end of 2020 due to the impact of COVID, with smaller charities (less than £1m) disproportionately affected. Whilst no one could have predicted a global pandemic, the truth is that many of these charities were operating hand to mouth prior to COVID, with very little reserves to fall back on when hard times hit.

There are just under 170,000 charities in the UK, with the top 20% accounting for 80% of overall income, leaving the vast majority fighting for a much smaller share. If we, and you, are to survive and thrive, we need to take our finances seriously, have difficult conversations, be diligent in our financial management and honest about our financial risk.

Now the good news

After that rather gloomy introduction, we can swiftly move on to what we can do to mitigate the challenges we face. It can seem an overwhelming task to try to turn around a charity in financial difficulty. Each of your organisations will have different purpose, services, funders, cost base and starting position, but the important elements of financial management are common to us all.

Depending on your circumstances, you may tackle these in any order, but they are all important and have been significant in our journey to financial stability.

The importance of the finance team

When I joined SJOG the finance team sat in a large room at the end of the corridor. The door was permanently closed 'to keep it quiet', and no other colleagues except the receptionist delivering post or the odd IT visit, dared to pass the threshold. By the end of the first week I had jammed the door open, visited everybody in the building and made sure they knew finance were there, there to help, as is the purpose of the charity

Finance was seen as a 'back office' team, adding up numbers, generally complaining and delivering bad news. Even more worryingly is that the finance team actually saw themselves that way too. They lacked purpose, direction and had lost sight of the value they added or could and should add.

It is so important that finance, and other support functions, are seen as integral parts of the charity, contributing towards delivering on purpose and there to help not hinder, colleagues in delivery. Central to achieving this vision of finance are two things: the team having a clear purpose and strategy, and the communication of this to the wider organisation.

> **Questions to ask yourself**
> - Does our finance team have a strategy, which supports the charity's strategy?
> - Do the team feel they are contributing?
> - Does our organisation understand what finance does and why?
> - Is the finance team integral to, and valued by, the wider organisation?

Set a finance strategy

Setting a finance strategy delivers on a couple of key objectives.

Firstly, in setting it with the team, it builds morale and provides focus and common direction. It illustrates the clear value the team can bring in supporting the organisational strategy, and provides a reference point from which to identify achievement. Some of the team will require more support and encouragement than others in contributing to the process but it is worth the effort when the outcome is a cohesive, energised and motivated team.

Secondly, the strategy becomes a great tool in communicating with the rest of the charity. It sets out why finance are here, what they do and why they do it, and galvanises the relationships between finance and other departments, especially operations.

Our finance strategy had nine key strands as shown in Figure 9, each supported by targeted actions and goals. Each action or target is connected to supporting the organisational strategy and the team have a clear line of sight to this. This may help you in starting to think about how you set your own finance team strategy and what priorities you have. It doesn't have to be perfect, and it will have several iterations over time, but it needs to be owned by the team - get it up on the wall, use it as a screen saver and regularly review the actions to highlight progress. When you have a long way to go in turning round a charity, it can be easy to lose track of what you have achieved along the way and the difference the team has made and this is critical to keep everyone motivated. In challenging times, it is even more important to recognise improvement and celebrate the good.

> **Questions to ask yourself.**
> - Are we tracking against tasks and recognising progress?
> - Does our team feel like they are achieving?

Fig 9. The SJOG Finance Model

Communicate the strategy

In the first year I presented this strategy at our conference and explained exactly what we were trying to do and why. I also introduced each of the team personally, to put faces to the names, and what their key responsibilities were and provided a brief overview of the charity's challenging financial position and where we were trying to get to. The feedback was phenomenal and completely reset the tone for finance/operations relationship. In addition, getting the whole team out and about in your services, meeting people, communicating the strategy, reinforcing the willingness to support and help, and deliver on purpose is really powerful. The importance of the visibility of the team in the charity cannot be overstated. It continually underlines the messaging and builds strong relationships but also reminds the team why they are here, why what they do it important and how they can contribute.

Finance is not a secret to be kept behind closed doors, nor is it to be made out to be complicated, separate, or scary.

> ## Questions to ask yourself.
> - Do we communicate with the wider organisation?
> - Do people know the team and what they do?
> - How could we communicate more to build relationships?

Take care

Look after your team, whether it be a team of 20 or 1. Finance can be a lonely place in challenging times and the finance team are sometimes an unfairly easy target for people's frustrations.

Ask yourself, are they the right people in the right roles? Are they happy to work for the organisation? Some work on role definition and team structure can go a long way in improving how the team works and feels.

The building of a finance strategy definitely helps morale along with having regular meetings and informal chats, but it is important not to forget the individual and recognising their value and needs.

Regular supervisions or one-to-ones are important to keep in touch with how they are feeling, to provide one-to-one support and gauge how content colleagues are. It is an opportunity to set direction and objectives and give credit for a job well done.

Whilst colleagues are working hard to get the charity back on track they need to feel valued and invested in. When cash is short you must be creative around ways of offering training and development for example, use any funding pots you have access to and explore low cost online and internal training options. We will explore this more in the People chapter but look for low cost or cost neutral ways to offer additional benefits when options on pay increases are limited.

What's the problem?

Understanding why a charity is in financial difficulty is the first step in turning things around. It is likely that there will be multiple issues contributing to a deficit or cash shortfall and it is important that all are identified, prioritised and tackled, in order to improve. You will need to be honest about where you are and the risks the charity faces. Being overly optimistic with the board will not help to address where things are going wrong. Building trust with the board is important, they are after all legally responsible for the finances of the charity. Whether the news is good or bad, the board need to be sighted on the facts. Consistently providing accurate and clear information will provide comfort to trustees/directors that someone in the organisation has a clear grip on the finances and that they are being presented with a true picture along with a plan for resolving issues.

Cash is King

As we mentioned in the opening chapter, the basics of good charity financial management are not complicated. The old adage 'cash is king' is never far from my mind; when the king is in trouble, the kingdom is in trouble. Organisations, both profit-driven and charitable, fail when they run out of cash and cannot pay their liabilities as they fall due. In some cases, this can be despite delivering 'profitable' services.

Look carefully and honestly at your cash position. Do you have enough cash to pay your liabilities day to day, week to week, month to month? Forecast at least six months ahead, longer if you can, and be realistic, then pessimistic. Imagine worst-case scenarios and play them out through your cash flow. How long can you continue if your funding reduces by 10%, 20%, 50%? What would you do in these scenarios to protect the charity? The more analysis you can do the better, be rigorous. Putting one's head in the sand is not a financial strategy I would recommend.

- Be open with your senior colleagues and your board about the cash position; explain the shortfalls, the likely pinch points.

There is little stress comparable to that associated with financial problems, therefore it is important to share that load.

- Use the forecasting and what if scenarios to create a short-term action plan to address the most urgent matters, with additional actions for the medium and longer term.

- Attack working capital first, can you stretch terms with suppliers and work hard on credit control, so you have money in your bank sooner? Where you need to cut costs to give some breathing space, do so.

- Review overheads robustly, line by line, challenge costs and make savings where you can, negotiate with suppliers or tender for new ones, consider restructuring if the overhead staffing burden is too high.

There is a need to be supportive and solution driven, understanding, and acknowledging the needs of the communities and people we are here to support, but we need to be a proactive, challenging companion for our colleagues at times, question their logic and decision-making.

Questions to ask yourself

- What does our cash flow look like?
- Have we stress tested our cash flow? What ifs?
- What are our contingency plans?
- Do we have alternative funding sources?
- How much cash is tied up in debtors?
- Can we agree to pay suppliers on longer terms?
- Challenge overheads, source cheaper suppliers, place a moratorium on non-critical spending

What's really going on?

Following the cash analysis then is the time to get to the root causes of the financial problems. In my experience, these can be wide and far-reaching, and whilst there may be quick wins, some will take much longer to resolve and some you may choose to accept and live with.

Overheads

Overheads is an easy place to start and can deliver early savings. Over time, it is almost inevitable that overheads creep up in an organisation and now is the time to have a critical review of them. It is worth checking where responsibility for overhead spend lies. You may find that there is a distinct lack of control of overheads, a culture of renewing and not pushing back on costs, because we are a charity. I have found that my 'cold hearted' private sector background has paid off here! Don't be afraid to challenge suppliers, ask for a discount (you invariably get something!), better terms, alternative quotes. Customers have choice, be a proper customer. We want to have good relationships with suppliers and treat them fairly, but it is not uncharitable to try to get best value, in fact, that is exactly our duty.

Responsibility for spending is a key control to tackle which can have significant positive effects. Making sure all overhead spend is covered within a budget and the accountability of a budget holder is an effective tool in managing costs. We will discuss budgeting in more detail later but challenge budget holders to stay within budgeted levels and make savings where possible. Non-budgeted expenditure should require additional sign off through levels of approval using a delegated authorities matrix.

If your cash flow shortfalls are serious, you may consider a spending moratorium until you are in a more comfortable position. This sends a message that things are serious, will bring some control and allow for more accurate forecasting.

Questions to ask yourself

- Are there overheads you can manage without?
- Are you getting best value from suppliers?
- Do you have clear approval levels for spending?

Operational finances

If you are lucky enough to have systems that provide lots of data to analyse, you are at an immediate advantage in trying to understand what is contributing to financial difficulty. A thorough review of the data will highlight which services are underperforming and for how long this has been the case, and which areas are of most concern.

In most cases however, we are not so lucky in the quality and quantity of data we have access to and need to take a broader approach.

Whilst working to breakdown the underlying performance through financial analysis, it is important to simultaneously work closely with operational colleagues, budget holders and managers. Talk with them about the details of their services, how they are funded, how fees or income is acquired, how they staff their services, review all the costs they incur. Ideally, all this work would be done personally in their location where they feel most confident rather than an appointment at head office. It is important to reinforce that this is a means to helping the service to become sustainable. It is not an interrogation or fault-finding mission, rather it is another opportunity for building relationships, understanding the service better and truthfully, and most finance colleagues really benefit from seeing the other side of the fence.

In building trust and rapport with operational managers, you can really start to unpick the detail and uncover the key factors driving poor financial performance. In our case it was a combination of lots of factors including over-providing against some commissioned services, under-providing others, inefficient rotas, ineffective or lack of fee negotiations with funders, lack of non-staff spending control. In your organisation, there will no doubt be a similar raft of common factors at play with some or all affecting each service.

You may not have the luxury of completing all of the analysis before deciding what action to take first. Cash demands may drive early decisions or you may uncover issues that require immediate action. In any event, there will be surprises as you go along the journey that will throw you off course and need correction. The list this investigation generates may seem onerous at the start. Work through it in detail and identify risks, priorities, quick wins and those actions that will have the greatest positive impact for the charity. I would recommend fully reviewing with your senior team and board and obtain their sign off and support for the plan ahead, engender collective responsibility in making the changes to turn things around. Tackling these issues will take time and resources, and it is important to be open with the board about this. Agreeing the issues to tackle, with some indicative timescales provides another way to measure progress and impact which you can present to the board, and, in a more streamlined way, to the operations managers and wider colleagues, ensuring a high level of visibility throughout the charity.

- Talk to managers and interrogate the financials, find out what is going on
- Create a plan of action - prioritise
- Be open and agree with board

Hard decisions

In my previous life in the private sector, profit-driven decisions were made continually. Deciding to bid for higher value electrical safety consultancy vs low margin maintenance programmes is easy; it makes good financial sense, we have the scarce expertise via the right people for high value work, and the more generic, less profitable maintenance work will just go to another supplier. Easy.

In the charity world, these decisions are much more difficult. One thing I have been able to 100% count on in this sector is the passion of the managers delivering services.

When you visit a service, providing community benefit with lovely colleagues, it makes it that much more difficult to decide not to continue with the provision. Although an absolute last resort, deciding to close a service or discontinue an offering, is an option that is critical to consider.

In situations where you are operating at your most efficient and cannot negotiate additional funding or income, it may be that you need to make a difficult decision for the benefit of the whole charity. Can you afford to provide the service? As a charity with finite resources, we need to be clear on providing the most benefit we can and sometimes that means saying goodbye to services that others are better placed to deliver. As just one of the 170,000 UK charities, we don't have an automatic right to exist and to continue, and so we have to make sure we are using the charity's resources to best effect and in the most sustainable way.

> **Questions to ask yourself**
> - What aspects of our delivery are proving impossible to fund 100%?
> - Can we afford to provide the services we offer?
> - Are others better placed to provide?
> - Where might our resources be used more efficiently?
> - Are there any services which are not furthering the purpose of the charity?

Being open

There is a way to explain the organisational financial challenges to colleagues at all levels without sending them into panic. A problem highlighted with a plan to solve it is much less daunting, but still serves to make colleagues aware. In difficult times, there is often a feeling amongst colleagues that things are not going well so it is better to be clear and avoid rumours. In my experience, talking more openly to colleagues at all levels across the charity about our finances has had a positive effect. People feel informed, better able to understand higher-level decision-making and it has had a positive impact on the financial decisions they have made in their services.

Budgeting

Transforming the way that budgeting had previously been done in our organisation has been one of the most important ways we have gained control over the financial performance of the charity.

Historically, inaccurate budgets had been put together by senior management and issued to managers. These were completed late, with little reference to any business plan for the charity, and not surprisingly there was very little accountability or buy in from other managers in the charity. The budgets were meaningless and performance against budget was poor across the charity.

Your budget should be the financial translation of the business plan for the charity, you should not be writing one without the other.

We decided to take a bottom-up approach to budgeting, with managers submitting business plans and accompanying budgets for approval. Now, I am not going to say this worked seamlessly first time around! There was a lot of work in educating managers on planning and budgeting, a lot of hand holding time from finance and several iterations, but each subsequent budget round saw improvement.

The value in spending time with managers to help with budgeting was three fold. Firstly, and importantly, it further improved relationships between finance and operations. Managers realised we were there to help and support.

Secondly, by working through the business plan and budget template in detail, managers really began to truly understand the finances of their service and the finance team uncovered opportunities to increase income and save costs.

Thirdly, because the budgets were developed with manager input, there was a high level of buy in and therefore accountability. This was a clear move away from finance 'telling' to finance 'collaborating', and it was welcomed.

It is fair to say that the first year definitely threw up some anomalies, costs that were under budgeted or missed, provisions that were overlooked, however this was a learning curve and the subsequent years have been much improved. Managers are now familiar with the business planning process and increased confidence means they are coming up with create ideas to improve or expand services.

Budgeting is more accurate and managers are familiar with the templates. Below is a typical timeline for our budget process. It's worth mentioning that our financial year runs from January to December.

Fig 10. The SJOG Budget Process

July 2020	• Service reviews completed with operations and finance • Managers introduced to the 2021 budget process • 2021 budget templates issued to department/service managers
August 2020	• Operations managers work with department/service manager on the preparation of the 2021 business plan and 2021 budgets
September 2020	• Operational manager present portfolio budgets to COO and CFO • Budget finalised and consolidated by finance • Final draft budgets agreed for presentation to Senior Team
October 2020	• Completed business plans and budgets presented to the Senior Team for agreement
November 2020	• Budget sign off by Finance, Audit and Risk Committee
December 2020	• Budget sign off by Trustees

Questions to ask yourself

- Do we have a well-planned business planning and budgeting process?
- Can we provide easy templates for our managers and commit time to education and confidence building?

Review and accountability

Quality budgeting with manager ownership facilitates meaningful review throughout the year. This is the part that most improves financial results. Because there is a commitment to the budget by managers, they want to deliver on it. When the budget is finalised, finance and operations are completely aligned and in agreement having produced a budget the manager is content to deliver on.

When the service is underperforming financially, we can quickly spot it through monthly reviews, and discuss ways to mitigate or rectify with the manager.

Identifying issues early stops them from becoming problems and there is a lower likelihood that service performance becomes out of control.

For challenging services, you may review performance monthly, for those of less concern perhaps quarterly. This requires the finance team to issue reporting regularly and facilitate meetings but is invaluable in monitoring performance. When a service gets into difficulty, the review may be escalated to include more senior members of the team but key to this is the spirit of working together to resolve, helping each other and being on the same team. It is critical to reinforce this, especially when performance isn't good.

Being a good finance partner to service managers means supporting them when times are difficult, working on solutions together and sharing the burden.

Questions to ask yourself

- Do we regularly review financial performance with managers?
- Could we work closer to spot problems and work on improvements as a cohesive team?

What now?

Assuming you can make the changes above to get back onto an even financial keel and the pressure on cash flow eases, what is the role of finance now?

Well, all of the things we have talked about so far need to continue in some form. Cash flow management, cost management, spending and decision making controls, team development, budgeting, income generation and negotiation, financial review - all these aspects need to continue to keep us on track and honest about the charity's financial health. It is all too easy to become complacent and drop back into old ways so we must ensure controls are in place to monitor.

Reflecting on what has led to your charity being in financial distress should guide where you direct financial resources in the future. Whether it was a lack of stability due to insufficient reserves, low levels of liquidity to cover shortfalls in cash, poor financial management of services and decision making regarding new services, put safeguards in place to make sure these mistakes are not repeated.

Reserves

Building reserves so that the charity is in a position to weather a storm is critical to the sustainability of the organisation. When services are operating in surplus and you are able to start to build strength into the balance sheet, it is important to keep in mind the challenges that might lay ahead and develop a robust reserves policy. Give the charity time to recover and rebuild before trying to expand too far.

New services

Being of more help is an obvious driver of all charities, especially when there is so much need. However, taking on services without thinking carefully about the financial impact is foolish and is likely one of the reasons why you may have ended in difficulty in the past. Have a robust bid/no bid policy, look at financials in detail and only take on services where you have full visibility of risk and can be sure of financial sustainability.

Whilst caution is urged after achieving stability, it is however, a point at which you can start to look to the future and how finance plays a part in building a sustainable platform for growth and in reviewing and taking opportunities. Having control at a tactical level creates the headroom for a strategic look ahead, towards sustainable development. It is where we got to after two years hard work, and it is a nicer place to be.

> **Reflection**
> - Your budget should be the financial translation of the business plan for the charity, you should not be writing one without the other.
> - Being a good finance partner means supporting colleagues when times are difficult.

References

Pro Bono Economics, 2020.Covid Charity Tracker Survey Results. London https://www.probonoeconomics.com/Pages/Category/policy-and-research?Take=48

Good Work

The role of people and the importance of community in helping your organisation flourish

What you will find here:
- Delivering purpose through people
- Human flourishing and bus stops
- The right people on the bus

Leadership is all about people

"Leadership is all about people. It is not about organisations. It is not about plans. It is not about strategies. It is all about people motivating people to get the job done. You have to be people centred."

Colin Powell

So, in determining what motivates our colleagues, let's start by focusing on you, by asking you three questions.

1. **Would you like to work for a successful organisation?**
   By that I mean an organisation that delivers on its purpose and does so in a sustainable way so that it can continue to be of benefit into the future. Obviously, the alternative to this binary choice is working in an organisation that is not successful and isn't around in the future. Well?

   Working in a successful organisation is great but there is one thing better than working for a successful organisation and that is knowing that you contributed to the success.

2. **Would you like to do a good job in a role which is meaningful?**
   Nobody in the history of the world has ever said that what they want from their life is to work in mind-numbing job that makes no difference at all. That's not to say that people don't do these jobs, it's just no-one has ever set out to work in a mind-numbing job that makes no difference.

   I have some experience in this. When I was at university, I took a summer job working for a company that put up big marquees at events. These were not your average marquees but were so large that they had two floors and had big patio doors that were used to keep the VIP guests comfortable no matter what the elements were doing outside.

The company had teams of skilled people to take them to venues, build them safely and then once all the canapes had been eaten and the wine drunk, take them down. Obviously, they let me as a 19-year-old student nowhere near this.

However, once the event was over the mud splattered marquees would be taken back to the warehouse to be cleaned and stored until they were next needed. This is where I came in.

My role was to work with a colleague to lift the patio doors out of the storage racks, take them across the huge warehouse to an area where we would clean them, and then haul them back across the warehouse and place them in the racks.

It was simple, repetitive, heavy work that a student could be entrusted with. I stayed because it paid reasonably well, but it was work that was made pointless by the fact that the warehouse was dusty, so by the time the doors were taken out for their next event they were covered in a thick layer of dust and had to be cleaned again. I worked the six weeks and took the wage but was ready to leave weeks before the end of the summer.

The pointlessness of work has been used in prisons and camps to demoralise those held within them. Whether it's carrying a stone from one place to another just to have someone else carry it back or digging a hole then filling it in again. These are tasks to occupy people's time, but it's designed to be demeaning. If you want an example of this, then the film 'The Castle' with Robert Redford has a great one.

Fortunately for me my life is no longer full of patio doors. After university I started working in charities directly supporting people. I believed that I was good at helping people to do the things that they wanted to do but needed support with. I liked my role. It was worthwhile and when I went home at the end of the day, I could point to all of the things that had made a difference in someone's life.

These days I don't have that immediate feedback. I spend a lot of time talking about how we will fund the things we do, or plan for what we should do next. I talk about how we can change the systems we work in, and spend an awful lot of time thinking about how we can make this a reality. It's work that takes a long time to come to fruition and some days I go home wondering if what I did today was worthwhile, but there are other days when we secure funding or open a new service when the sense of achievement is huge!

I was thinking about this when driving to work and each day I hope that I'll laugh with people, have interesting discussions about things that matter and go home at the end of the day feeling that what I've done is worthwhile.

Theodore Roosevelt succinctly said:

"Far and away the best prize that life offers is the chance to work hard at work worth doing."

The idea was not new in FDR's time and it predates the previous comments from John Lewis in the 1920s, but it's much older than that. It all begins in antiquity with Aristotle who 2,400 years ago said that we're at our happiest when we are doing good work and doing it well. I am of course paraphrasing because my ancient Greek is not all that it could be.

Even Herzberg when he stopped worrying about his hygiene said that:

"If you want someone to do a good job then give them a good job to do."

I like that. It's our responsibility as leaders to give our colleagues a good job to do and then support them to do it well.

3. **Would you like to feel valued at work?**

No, it's not a trick question. The answer is as obvious as you think it is, but I'm asking this because of the Golden Rule.

The Golden Rule occurs in each of the world's religions. It's that you should treat others the way you want to be treated yourself. Do you want to be treated fairly, with compassion and respect? Enough said.

What's interesting to me is that it's easy to treat people well and for people to feel that they are valued and treated with respect. It works every day on even the smallest of interactions. If we smile at people when we meet them, then they are more than likely to smile back.

In your interactions as a leader in your organisation you set the tone, building the environment that your colleagues work in. You determine the way that things are done around here. Smile at people, laugh, be respectful and be human and that will set the culture, which is still my favourite way of saying 'the way that we do things around here'.

The great thing is that if you take care of your colleagues well, they will take care of each other, and in so doing better deliver on the purpose of your charity, which is of course why you employed them in the first place.

The value of good work

Receiving a fair wage for the work that you do is important but there is more to feeling valued than how much you are paid. For me it's about being part of something bigger and knowing that your contribution not only makes a difference but is seen to make a difference.

It is about being thanked for good pieces of work that you do, but it's also being pulled up on those occasions when your work hasn't quite reached the desired standard. We all have those days. You'll know when your work is not your best and it's good to know that the quality of your work matters enough that it matters to others as well.

At SJOG we help our colleagues to feel valued, but setting clear expectations and then supporting them to achieve this.

We're clear about our expectations and what 'doing a good job' looks like. We audit each of our services every month and track the performance of teams over time, offering support when needed so that our colleagues can achieve the standards that we set. We also publish the scores of each of the service's quality audits. We have nothing to hide and a little bit of competition between teams can be a positive thing!

We ask our teams to go further and do more, even if it's outside of their comfort zone. I know my team love it when I offer them opportunities to stretch themselves (if not at the time, then later!).Knowing that someone else believes in your ability even when you are not sure communicates that you are valued and trusted.

We remind our colleagues often that the work they do is worth doing and thank them for the work that they do. A thank you is a simple thing, but it's effective and we find other ways to show our colleagues that they are valued.

Whilst I said that value isn't just about receiving a fair wage for the work that you do, it is important. I was at a conference listening to someone talking about how to value your team, and he said it's not difficult and went on to list:

1. You give support to your team and listen to them
2. You give them the tools that they need to do their job well
3. You pay them a proper wage
4. You give them the benefits that you can afford

All that seems sensible enough, but then he said," ...then give them a little bit more." This was followed by a pause for dramatic effect and then he continued, "...until it hurts." Now I'm with him most of the way but I'm not sure about 'give until it hurts', it sounds slightly masochistic, but it did lodge it in my mind, so I guess it served its purpose.

The benefit of good work

You need to take care of the people in your organisation, but this valuing of people is not entirely altruistic. There may be a moral imperative to treat others as you would like to be treated, but there is also a business imperative and sound management theory that sits behind this.

J Stacey Adams' equity theory is often shown as a set of scales with a basket of things that people get out of a role (the value) on one side and the things that they put into a role on the other. If they are balanced then people are content, if they feel they are putting in more than they are getting out then dissatisfaction creeps in.

But the things that people value are not the same as they were in the 1960s when the model was first developed. LinkedIn's 2021 Workplace Learning Report showed that 76% of Generation Z learners believe that learning is a key part to their career success. Furthermore, it recommended that organisations need to ensure proper mapping exercises to learning, accessibility to content, ongoing opportunities, relevant communities for connection, ongoing engagement, ongoing workplace support and good policies and procedures.

The other things that we found were valued are giving people a day to volunteer in another charity or community project of their choice, and receiving a hand-written card at Christmas, which are both all about seeing people, and seeing them as individuals.

On financial benefits colleagues have said that they have valued an opportunity to save via a credit union and Information brochures that we've produced on reducing their monthly expenditure. As I said it's not always about increasing income and cash bonuses (but that's good too!).

Creating good work

This is your role, to create an environment where people want to come to work and can do a meaningful job well. In the 1970s Greenleaf spoke about servant leadership, which captured this view that leaders are here to help their colleagues succeed. This was possibly building on the work of Kant, but whichever philosophy you follow, the maths work.

As a leader in the charity, I make choices. I can choose to work on being more efficient in my role, or I can help my 560 colleagues to be more efficient in theirs. How do you choose? Well which makes more difference in delivering on our purpose, my being 1% more effective in my role or making a change that means my colleagues can spend 1% more of their day delivering on the purpose. I know which feels like a bigger win for the charity.

It's within my gift, and yours, to make systems easier for our colleagues, to provide them with the technology that streamlines their roles. It's also in our gift to provide more opportunities to be of use by providing them with experiences that stretch them so that they can develop their skills and knowledge.

Can I suggest that as a leader in your organisation you take time to remove what blocks and do more of what rocks, and if you are not sure of what rocks and what blocks then ask your colleagues. We'll restate you may know a lot, but you don't know everything. It's not your role and you are not Google, so listen to the people around you they know more about their roles than you do. Value their views and opinions.

Make time to have conversations with people, and as covered in the previous chapters they will share their keyholes of truth which all adds to your understanding of the gestalt.

Would you like to work with skilled and knowledgeable people?

I know I do. I love working with the team that has written this book. Over the past four years we've worked hard and tackled difficult situations together with each of us bringing a distinct set of complementary skills to the charity. I know that I couldn't do their roles, but I respect that they can and the professional skills they bring to bear for the benefit of the charity.

I also like them. As a team we're harmonious. We don't always all agree, but we can disagree and challenge each other knowing that at our heart each of us is trying to make the organisation more successful.

In terms of the people, I want to (and do) work with, I value their complementary professional skills and knowledge, a work ethic, a focus on purpose and an ability to disagree positively.

More widely in considering who I want to work with there are four areas that I think should be focused on:

- Recruiting the right people
- Losing the right people
- Growing the right people
- Retaining the right people

Recruiting the right people

There used to be a poster on the underground for a headhunting firm that said, 'if you think recruiting a professional is expensive, try recruiting an amateur'. It made me laugh when I first saw it and I think of it every time I start a recruitment process.

Recruitment is part of what we do, and there are real benefits in recruiting new skills and new ideas into the organisation, but it is also expensive. Now, I believe that every second that you spend on recruitment will save you hours in the future.

When recruiting I focus on attitude and skill rather than knowledge. That's because knowledge is the easiest thing to teach, building skills is more difficult but can be done; shifting attitudes is a whole lot harder and not usually a worthwhile investment of time and resources.

So, bring people into your charity who have the right attitudes, people who will add to the skills of your team, and there's a third point, people who you would like to work with. That final point is really important and very rarely spoken about.

When I recruit, I ask myself three questions:

1. Will this person be able to do the job?
2. Will this person fit in?
3. Will this person stay long enough to make the investment in the recruitment process worthwhile?

To expand further, having the technical skills and the knowledge to do the role is important. We employ people into roles that require very little pre-knowledge; they arrive enthusiastically with the right set of soft skills, and we train them in the specifics of their role over time, supporting them and providing all the skills and knowledge that they need. That's great, its expected and we plan accordingly, but we also recruit into specialist roles and supervisory and management roles, and we expect people to bring all of the soft skills and a set of specialist skills and knowledge that make the organisation better than it is at the moment.

The second point is really important. Will this person fit in? Let's be clear at the outset that this isn't about cloning yourself in the interview process or only bringing in people who look and sound like the rest of the organisation but there are some non-negotiables.

I once interviewed a person for a role to support men who had recently been released from prison. The role was about change and providing people with other options. The candidate said that he was happy to provide support, but his view was that this should always be focused on the short term as 'a leopard can't change its spots'. His belief was the men that he would be supporting would be heading back to prison soon.

He didn't get the job.

On paper he was a great candidate with relevant qualifications and experience, but he didn't fit with the approach that we had, so we went with someone who on paper wasn't as strong but shared the values of the charity.

Shared values is one of the seven 'S's in the McKinsey 7S model and it sits right at the very heart of their excellent diagram.

Peters and Waterman (1982) developed the model for management consultancy McKinsey through interviewing 62 successful businesses. The seven traits they identified were:

1. A bias for action
2. Close to customers
3. Autonomy and entrepreneurship
4. Productivity through people
5. Stick to the knitting
6. Simple form, lean staff
7. Simultaneous loose, tight properties

Tom Peters said that whilst the model they had created was sensible, understandable and grounded in good research, it was not memorable and so, "With a bit of stretching, cutting and fitting we ended up with 7 variables starting with S and a logo."

It's so memorable that it's become a staple in thousands of management lectures and books (including this one!).

Fig 11. The McKinsey 7S Model after Peters and Waterman (1982)

The third question we ask ourselves is, "Will this person stay long enough to make the investment in the recruitment process worthwhile?"

We don't expect people to stay forever, and there is an explanation used in the charity to explain what it is that we do, and to put a frame of reference on this question.

As a charity we are not a destination for the people we are here to support. No one grows up with an ambition to be supported by us. We are a bus stop, people come to us. We give them time to take a breath, work out where they want to go next, and then we make sure that they have everything they need to make the next step in their journey. This is as true for our colleagues as it is for the people that we are here to support. Some may stay for a year, some for 20 or 30 years, but either way we are unlikely to be a final destination.

Lisa, our chief operating officer, gets right to the heart of the matter when she asks candidates the question, 'How can we help you to be successful?'

But if that requires more explanation, then she goes on to explain that this is unlikely to be the last job you ever have so whilst you are in this job, what can we do to make sure that you are ready to take your next step?

It's a simple question but it shows real interest in the journey that our colleagues are on. It's not all about us, it underlines that we are here to help and it makes sure that when colleagues arrive we already know how to tailor their induction into the charity.

Growing the right people

Every one of our colleagues is brilliant in their own way. We'll support colleagues to excel by doing more of what they are good at, as well as supporting the areas where they require a bit more help. We do this through our learning pathways.

The learning pathways are a way of ensuring that every person is competent in their role and that we have the evidence to support this assertion.

We recognise that colleagues join us from a diverse range of industries and even those who have previously done what we do may not have done this in the way that we do it.

The learning pathways provide a record of competence, which is useful for our regulators, and when things go wrong, as they will, we have evidence to show that we have done what we needed to do to ensure that our colleagues have the necessary skills and experience. The fact that people are well trained and knowledgeable also means that things are likely to go wrong less often and with less impact.

Our learning pathway looks like this.

Fig 12. The SJOG Learning Pathways

The model was designed in a way to move away from a layered hierarchy, to reflect that we are all important, much like the cogs within a clock's mechanism. Take one of these out and the clock stops working.

The learning pathways are built around the needs of the charity. We started by understanding our purpose, developed a strategy and then identified the learning opportunities that we needed to develop so that we could deliver on our strategy. We now provide over 140 mandatory and specialist courses. We don't deliver them all in-house but instead these have tapped into the networks around us. These have helped us to shape specialist training further, whilst also developing partnerships for the future.

We've come a long way. We moved beyond the 'one and done' training courses, and have built a culture that leverages learning, development and even better opportunities. The learning pathways develop over time to reflect the aspirations and expectations of the charity's beneficiaries and colleagues themselves.

Everyone across the charity, no matter what their role completes the same charity induction and mandatory courses, with the aim that we have a shared understanding of the role of the charity, our values and our aspirations. This is the theoretical underpinning of our culture and links back to the McKinsey 7S framework.

Whether colleagues are at the start of their career, stepping into management or in senior roles, there is an option to complete the pathway from their role and then reach across into other areas to stretch their learning, and encourage their curiosity. There is no restriction to this because we want people who are interested, knowledgeable and skilled right across the charity. Each role has its own pathway, and each colleague is required to complete this but they are not limited to this.

We've said before that the world continues to change and so the roles that we have in our charity will have to change to meet the changed world. Our learning pathways therefore continue to develop.

The offer has developed over the years and continues to evolve to meet our changing needs. An e-learning platform was developed, enabling flexible learning and both supported and encouraged the digital literacy within the charity. It also improved the record of training in the organisation and at the touch of a button we can know that we have 17,543 completed courses in this year.

Retaining the right people

A Forbes article in 2018 highlighted the correlation between employee development and organisational retention and we see that in our organisation.

Training is an investment and to be clear on this, like any investment we spend money and expect a return. That return to us is that there are better informed decisions being made at every level in the charity, that our culture is constantly reinforced through the training, and that we retain good people for a little bit longer.

It used to be the case when you went into a role and the expectation was that you would be in that role, or at least in that company, for life. Those days are long gone, and now anyone who is good at what they do will be in demand from your competitors and will move on, so retention is not about holding onto people, just holding onto people for a bit longer. Hopefully that means the cost of recruitment and the investment in training deliver a return.

People will join and be part of the organisation, and they will leave. Some will stay two years, some twenty, both are fine, but whilst colleagues are in the charity, we do everything that we can to support them to help them do their roles well, to grow and to flourish.

That support includes helping them to move on successfully. A successful move on has the benefit of widening our networks, and builds the reputation of the charity in the wider sector as people go on with their careers and say nice things about their experience of the charity.

In time we will all move on. In much the same way that we say that we are guests in the lives of the people that we support, we are also guests in this organisation. SJOG has stood for 140 years and the people that make up the charity now are just the latest in a long line of people who have contributed to the success of the charity. Our role as stewards of the charity is to ensure the ongoing success so that it can support people today and into the future, but we won't be the last. We are here for a time and then we'll move on; it's part of the natural order.

We'll always have turnover in our colleagues as people move onto further study, new opportunities or a new stage in their lives, but creating an environment where people want to stay longer, to contribute their skills and experience reduces the time, cost and disruption that recruitment and bringing new people into the charity brings.

In the year before I joined the charity there was a real problem with retention with turnover of people hitting 42%. Our recruitment processes were solid but as fast as we could bring people in through the front door, there were a larger number of people leaving through the back door.

In a bid to close the back door the LOVED programme was created.

LOVED is a promise to our colleagues, that as an organisation we will Live Our Values Every Day, and that means treating all of our colleagues with Hospitality, Compassion and Respect.

Practically that affects the way we word policies and what goes into them, and we try every day to ensure that our colleagues can flourish. We do this by giving colleagues the tools, the training and the trust that they need to deliver on the good work that they do.

It also means paying them properly and supporting them with the things that life throws at them. We offer support with mental health, with debt counselling and access to legal advice and health benefits. Our colleagues come to work to do good work, but this is only part of their lives, and if we can take some of the worries of daily life away then they can keep their minds on the tasks at hands. We live our values but there is also a real business benefit.

The LOVED programme

We offer a range of non-pay benefits. These have been developed with our colleagues as providing support to be well, physically, mentally, emotionally and financially.

Fig 13. The SJOG LOVED Rewards

The LOVED programme offers a range of non-pay benefits. As a charity the amount we can pay people as an income is constrained but we can help reduce our colleagues' expenditure. This includes paying for dentists and opticians, on gym memberships and even on the weekly shop.

It is not entirely altruistic but is valued and is often remarked on within our recruitment process by candidates.

The programme has a cost, but the monthly cost per person is tiny compared to the effect it as on underlining our values of Hospitality, Compassion and Respect.

LOVED is an approach that is larger than a range of non-pay benefits though.

It starts with recruitment and the welcome packs that we send out to people before they start and then with our induction programme.

Induction

Every induction is delivered with a member of the senior team. We are all part of the same organisation and it's an opportunity for the leaders within the organisation to be human and introduce themselves to all of our new colleagues.

Our induction also draws on the talent and genius of colleagues. Colleagues hear from their future peers what it's like to work at SJOG and hear some of the stories of how they make a difference. It's powerful and helps in setting expectations.

What is also powerful is asking our new colleagues, 'How can we help you have the best day' and then listening and acting on what we hear.

Portal

Belonging depends on knowing some of the same stuff. We address this from day one by providing access to our portal, which holds all of the information that anyone will need, and most importantly an excellent search function so that you can find what you need.

Information management has been an important area to focus. We spend time on this every year and colleagues are involved in making sure they have access to the resources and tools they need.

Learning and development networks

We've developed forums where colleagues come together and explore relevant topics of interest. Colleagues help shape how we work and share their keyholes of truth. These networks provide the opportunity to share best practice, reflect on learning and improve what we do.

Belonging

We work hard to build a sense of community and a sense of belonging.

It's easier for local organisations as people will naturally see each other more often, but for a national charity ensuring that people have regular touchpoints requires some work.

We provide a framework and what grows within this helps to shape the charity. We provide training, have our own internal social media where people can share things that are important to them, and we bring people together each year for conferences. It's a time to celebrate our successes and for colleagues to share their work. What we've found is that it shows the genius of our colleagues and enables everyone to understand the scale and range of the work that we do, and of course, the way we do this reinforces our values.

Recognising and celebrating outcomes

We ignite more contribution and commitment when we highlight the talent and achievements of our colleagues. It helps to keep morale high but also promotes the good work that we do. We have our internal Going the Extra Mile Awards (GEM Award) which celebrate the outcomes that colleagues achieve and highlights the impact of their contribution to the charity's purpose.

We also nominate our colleagues for national awards. All too often they see the work that they do every day as normal, but it is exceptional.

We promote private recognition which is often more detailed and held on a colleague's record. This can really motivate, engage and reinforce the values of the organisation. Feedback from colleagues has indicated that this is at least as beneficial as public recognition.

Competency frameworks

Our competency framework is aligned with our purpose and key strategic messages.

The framework was co-designed with our colleagues. It's a great way of measuring where you are in your own development and helps draw out the areas that may need further development. It sets out the values and behaviours that are consistent with SJOG and also helps in recruiting the 'right' people.

Engaging with IT

Not everyone in the team is a digital native but our colleagues are required to use tech every day. Ensuring that we invested in the digital literacy of our colleagues has meant that even the most resistant can take an active part in the community discussions and the sharing of stories within the charity.

Training to train

We keep saying that we have talented colleagues and we really do. We've supported colleagues to develop their knowledge and skills further by becoming trainers in their specialist areas of interest. It not only shares expertise across the charity, but shows our colleagues that we value what they bring to the charity.

We've found that this plays well with recruitment and retention, not only because it reflects that we respect our colleagues, but also that we invest in their development, and the development of the people they train.

Colleagues' survey

LOVED is a means of reinforcing our values, as well as holding the organisation to the same standard that we ask our colleagues to maintain.

We keep saying that we are all part of the same charity. We don't all work in the same building though, and making sure that we are supporting our colleagues in the way they want to be supported, rather than what we decide they want, requires some structure and thought.

We organise an annual survey, aligning the questions to the purpose and ask for feedback on chosen themes of interest. What is particularly important though is that we share the results with everyone even on the stuff that could be better. We also share what we plan to do off the back of this, and then later go back and share when this has been done.

Surveys are great, if you do something with them and share the learning and the actions, but beware, as the worst thing that you can do is ask people to tell you their opinions and then ignore them.

Belonging

Regular job changes are part of the way that the world is now. I can't help but feel that for the upsides of people being able to progress faster in their careers, being able to change roles or industries, and the shift of power from the employer to the employee (all good things!), we may have lost something.

Larger companies used to have pubs, social clubs and activities for people to come together outside of work. The John Lewis Partnership had their own hotel that was just for the people that worked at the John Lewis Partnership. So when you went on holiday you were socialising with people who were connected to the John Lewis Partnership.

Sure, it seems a bit weird to me, but back in less connected times when most people did not have access to a telephone, and the internet was waiting to be invented, the need for a sense of connection and belonging was still there. That was what John Lewis provided in creating a partnership, a sense of belonging to a community with a common purpose.

You may have picked up that I'm an admirer of John Spedan Lewis, the founder of the John Lewis Partnership. I think he was years ahead in his thinking.

He was gifted a loss-making department store by his father to keep him busy whilst he and his older son ran their main department store. He looked at the way his dad and brother ran their store and decided that it wasn't right that his dad and brother earned more than all of the other people working in store combined. So, he took a different approach and established the John Lewis Partnership, which we have previously shared has the ultimate purpose of:

> "The happiness of all its members through their worthwhile and satisfying employment in a successful business."

Two things here, the first is that this is about members not employees. Members choose to join a club or a society. In writing this back in the 1920s John Spedan Lewis recognised that each individual chose to join his business and why did they choose to do that? Well because it promised happiness, job satisfaction and being part of something worthwhile that will be successful, and as we've already established wouldn't we all want to be part of something that is a success rather than a failure?

Being part of something, belonging, is important, as we defined in the chapter on strategy. One of the things that make our life worthwhile is having someone who is important to us and being important to someone.

In your organisation you have a choice about how you view the people that choose to join it. You can view them as a resource, maybe even, as the cliché has it, as your greatest asset. Maybe they are just workers, clocking in, doing their job for the money you pay them, and then clocking out. Or maybe they are colleagues, people to learn from, who have chosen to join this community, and share a common purpose?

Colleagues that we develop may want to leave us and that's ok. We benefit from colleagues joining us from other charities, with a range of training and experience. Our training and development adds to the pool of talent in the sector, and if people go off and say nice things about the way we work and support people then that's good too as it adds to our credibility and reputation, and when people go and work in other charities then this extends our networks and reach.

Belonging to a wider community

We recognise that people have choices about where they work. Just in the charity sector in the UK there are 169,000 charities, most of them are tiny, with no paid employees, but even allowing for this there are, according to NCVO's excellent almanac, 950,000 people work in the charity sector.

This is about 3% of the total workforce in the UK, and in terms of a comparison, this is more than work in the police, armed forces and fire service combined.

Interestingly the people working in charities do not follow the patterns of people working in the public and private sectors. In the charity sector two thirds are women, almost a quarter (23%) say that they have a disability, and they tend to be older, and interestingly more white than their counterparts in other sectors.

At SJOG we have 639 paid colleagues. They help us to deliver on our purpose and many of them will have started their careers in other charities, or will progress their careers in other charities.

We also benefit from volunteers. Now I love volunteers, people who choose to give their time freely to a cause that they believe in. NCVO states that 16.3 million people over the age of 16 volunteered in the UK in 2021. That may be a single session or a longer-term commitment, but there's no doubt that civil society is stronger because of the willingness of people to freely get involved in their communities.

Volunteering is an area that's worthy of a book in its own right. Stating the obvious, volunteers contribute because they wish to, for no pay and that's a real benefit, but just because something is free at the point of use that doesn't mean that it has no cost.

To be clear volunteers are not a free resource. The management of volunteers needs investment, and the communication with and the inclusion of volunteers in decision-making is vital because they are a vital part of your community bringing skills, networks and knowledge to your communities. I've said before that your purpose is to make your organisation successful, and volunteers can help you to be more successful, but they need some support and valuing.

As for the worth of volunteers, as a charity you are likely to be led by a volunteer trustee board or management committee. They bring professional skills to provide governance and support to your charity, and they choose to do it for nothing.

Currently at SJOG we have a board that consists of two lawyers, the commercial director of one of UK's largest unions, a director of nursing, a person who led the global talent programme for one of the world's big four auditors, a director of one of the UK's leading house builders, a geophysicist, a physiotherapist and a teacher. These are highly skilled and knowledgeable individuals who lend their experience to the organisation because they believe in our purpose.

Volunteers are great and are valued in the sector and by society more generally, and we benefit from their involvement whilst they choose to remain, and should invest in them.

The investment we make in our colleagues, both paid and volunteer, is not lost when they leave us but is mostly retained in the wider charity sector. Just as we benefit from the training and skills that other organisations have invested in the people we recruit into the charity, we know that others will benefit from the training that we provide and that all adds into the common good.

At SJOG our purpose is often expressed as 'we're here to help', and for clarity that's not 'we're here to help the people that we offer services to' but it's a simple we're here to help, and that plays to a wider societal agenda to be of help where we can and that includes upskilling of the sector.

Letting the right people go

We take care of our colleagues; everyone has their own learning pathway; they are paid at a rate that is better than most in our sector, and we have a range of benefits and supports for them. We help support their health and wealth.

In return we expect our colleagues to do the role that they've been employed to do to the best of their abilities and with enthusiasm and care. We expect them to do their work, because if they don't then their colleagues or their line manager will need to step in and pick up the slack. That is why we say that we don't job share.

We all have our roles, we're all here to help each other get the work done, but to deliver effectively on our charitable purpose we need everyone to deliver on their areas of responsibility, and did I mention we don't job share.

We're a charity where people support people. We're naturally inclined to help people grow into roles and if people need a little more time and support, then we provide this, but our work is too important not to have the right people on the bus.

Jim Collins in his book 'Good to Great' spoke about getting the right people on the bus, and making sure that they were sat in the right seat. It's a useful analogy to focus on who you have in your charity and whether you have the right people, doing the right things to deliver on your purpose for, as was said in the chapter on purpose:

> "Everything that you do within your charity, when raising money, delivering services, employing people, training, paying bills are important only in so much as they help you deliver on that purpose."

Everyone in your organisation should have a role that helps to deliver on the purpose of the charity and if they don't why are they still here?

I said in the introduction that I've never started with a blank piece of paper; when we arrived in this charity there are already people in post. Some have become stars in the organisation, some have developed incrementally, and some people have left the charity.

When I started at SJOG as well as bringing in the team that's written this book, we said goodbye to 17 other roles in the charity. It's never easy to cut roles, but the focus on purpose helps.

It's one of those occasions when you need to take a deep breath, muster your courage and get on with it. Don't be afraid to prune your team so that the organisation can grow in the right way.

What is the right way? Well, it's the way that you and your board decides will best deliver on your organisational purpose.

It may sound brutal but don't hold on to people just because they've been in post for a while, or you like them. As a reminder, your only role is to help your organisation to be successful today and into the future.

As you make your changes, the world will continue to turn, continue to change, and so you need to shape your organisation to face tomorrow's challenges rather than what made it successful in the past. That includes only having the people in the organisation that can help you deliver on that.

Questions to ask yourself

- Do we want well skilled and knowledgeable people making decisions in our organisation?
- Do we have periodic reviews of our 'bus journey'. Are the right people still on the bus and in the right seats?

Reflection

- Our colleagues are important as they deliver on the purpose of the charity.
- We are a charity where people support people, and if people are not directly supporting the people we are here to serve, then they are supporting the people that are.
- As a leader our role is to make it easy as possible for colleagues to be successful by creating an environment where they can flourish.
- There is a moral imperative and a business imperative to treat our colleagues well.

References

Adams, J.S. (1963). Towards an understanding of inequity. The Journal of Abnormal and Social Psychology, 675, 422-436.

Brent, M. and Fiona Elsa Dent (2014). The leader's guide to managing people: how to usesoft skills to get hard results. Harlow, England: Pearson.

Carlson, R (1998). Don't sweat the small stuff ... and it's all small stuff. London: Hodder & Stoughton.

Collins, J. (2001).Good to Great: Why Some Companies Make the Leap ...and Others Don't. London: Random House. Herzberg F. 1966. Work and the nature of man; World Pub. Co., Cleveland, 1966

Peters, T.J. and Waterman, R.H. (1982) In Search of Excellence: Lessons from America's Best-Run Companies. Harper & Row, New York Pink, D.H. (2018). DRIVE: the surprising truth about what motivates us. S.L.: Canongate Books Ltd.

Roosevelt, T,1903, Labour Day speech.

Resources

Workplace Learning Report LinkedIn Learning's 5th Annual. (n.d.). [online] Available at:

https://learning.linkedin.corn/content/dam/me/business/en-us/amp/learning-solutions/images/wlr21/pdf/LinkedIn Learning Workplace-Learning-Report-2021-EN-1.pdf(accessed 26.06.21)

Building Better

The role of quality management systems in your long-term success

What you will find here:
- Could, should and must
- Meeting or exceeding customer expectation
- How do we know that we are good
- Embodying quality

Could, should and must

The work that goes on in charities is focused on public benefit. It's important, and so how do we make sure that our good work is good?

We said at the beginning that we have never started with a blank piece of paper. Charities exist in a societal, legal and regulatory context.

We must meet our legal requirements and our regulatory requirements. We should be able to meet societal expectations and we could choose to exceed these and become a beacon of how things could be.

You don't get to choose your legal and regulatory frameworks, but you do get to choose just how good you are and the level of quality that you are happy with.

Quality

Quality is one of those words that is hard to define but we know it when we see it.

A Michelin-starred meal in a great restaurant is quality, but then so is a McDonald's Happy Meal. In both cases the customer gets what they expect.

I once met with a funder and told her that she should fund our services because they were excellent. She stopped me and said that she spent public money and that the public purse couldn't afford 'excellent'. What she wanted was a good service that met all the statutory outcomes and an organisation that would work with her.

To put it another way she had decided that she wanted a reliable car that would get her to her destination, she didn't need that to be a Rolls Royce.

As an organisation you get to decide the level of quality that you will provide in your organisation. Is it important to you that you feed as many people as possible and hand out food in takeaway containers, or that everyone has the experience of sitting at a table with a knife and a fork and napkin because that values the individual. That will depend on your philosophy, but we are getting ahead of ourselves.

Can you define quality?

The best explanation of quality that I have ever read was by the Chartered Quality Institute:

> "Quality is an outcome - a characteristic of a product or service provided to a customer, and the hallmark of an organisation which has satisfied all of its stakeholders."

It's broad in description but in essence we are either 'meeting or exceeding customer expectations'.

W. Edwards Deming, working in the 1930s, was one step ahead of this when he stated that the customer definition of quality is the only one that matters.

Deming worked initially as an electrical engineer but then as an author, professor, statistician and management consultant. He became interested in whether statistical analysis could improve quality control and developed a 14-point set of principles. His principles have a track record, becoming the basis of Total Quality Management which helped to rebuild Japan after the Second World War.

What I like about this and other really great management models is that there is nothing surprising about them, they feel right and that's why they work. The challenge for you though is taking these obvious statements and working out how they fit into your organisation.

Deming's 14-point approach

Developed from University of Tennessee Health Science Centre

1. **Create a constant purpose toward improvement**
   - Plan for the long term.
   - Don't just do the same things better, also find better things to do.
   - Always have the goal of getting better.

2. **Adopt the new philosophy**
   - Embrace quality throughout the organisation.
   - Put your purpose (to be of benefit to your 'customers') first and design products and services to meet those needs.

3. **Stop depending on inspections**
   - Inspections are costly and unreliable - and they don't improve quality, they merely find a lack of quality.
   - Build quality into your process from start to finish.
   - Don't just find what you did wrong - eliminate the 'wrongs' altogether.
   - Use data to inform decisions to prove that the process is working.

4. **Use a single supplier for any one item**
   - Quality relies on consistency - the less variation you have in the input, the less variation you'll have in the output.
   - Analyse the total cost to you, not just the initial cost of the product.
   - Use quality statistics to ensure that suppliers meet your quality standards.

5. **Improve constantly and forever**
   - Continuously improve your systems and processes, and always try to be better.
   - Develop the people in your organisation through training and education.

6. **Use training on the job**
   - Train for consistency to help reduce variation.
   - Build a foundation of common knowledge.

7. **Implement leadership**
    - Expect your supervisors and managers to understand their workers and the processes they use.
    - Provide support and resources so that each person can do their best and that will be different for each person.

8. **Eliminate fear**
    - Allow people the right to be wrong to ensure that they're not afraid to express ideas or concerns.
    - The goal is to achieve high quality services so you're not interested in blaming people when mistakes happen, just to learn from them.
    - Use open and honest communication to remove fear from your charity. Be human.

9. **Break down barriers between departments**
    - Build the 'internal customer' concept - recognise that each department or function serves other departments that use their output. If you're not serving the people we are supporting then you should be supporting the people who are.
    - Build a shared vision.
    - Use cross-functional teamwork to build understanding and reduce adversarial relationships.

10. **Get rid of unclear slogans**
    - Let people know exactly what you want.
    - Don't let words and nice-sounding phrases replace effective leadership. Outline your expectations, and then praise people face-to-face for doing good work.

11. **Eliminate management by objectives**
    - Be careful what you measure. Deming said that production targets encourage high output and low quality.
    - Provide support and resources so that production levels and quality are high and achievable.
    - Measure the process rather than the people behind the process.

12. **Remove barriers to pride of workmanship**
    - Allow everyone to take pride in their work without being rated or compared.
    - Treat people equally as partners rather than competing with other workers for monetary or other rewards. Over time, the quality system will naturally raise the level of everyone's work to an equally high level.

13. **Implement education and self-improvement**
    - Encourage people to learn new skills to prepare for future changes and challenges.
    - Build skills to make your colleagues more adaptable to change, and better able to find and achieve improvements.

14. **Make 'transformation' everyone's job**
    - Improve your overall organisation by having each person take a step toward quality.
    - Analyse each small step, and understand how it fits into the larger picture.
    - Use effective change management principles to introduce the new philosophy and ideas in Deming's 14 points.

How is quality defined in your organisation?

What Deming called the philosophy of quality is traditionally focused upon the development and implementation of an organisational-wide culture that emphasises certain principles.

We've touched on this already in the chapter on Purpose and the 'what' and 'how' of the charity, as defined in our values.

Fig 14. SJOG Values

HOSPITALITY	COMPASSION	RESPECT
Hospitality... is offering a welcome to those in any kind of need. Every day, we say 'come in, you are very welcome' and every day we are inspired by the strength, humanity and hospitality of the people that we work alongside.	Compassion... the support that we offer is underpinned by the active gift of kindness, caring and a demonstration of being willing to help.	Respect... we respect the dignity of each person, to choose how they live and our support and care does not degrade a person's inherent dignity.

For us our quality is shown in our ability to live our values, and we have a programme for our colleagues called LOVED, Living Our Values Every Day.

Organisational values demonstrate ways of doing things and in SJOG we often say, "The values on the wall match the values on the floor."

Our values all have people at their centre and therefore our philosophy of quality also has people at the centre of everything we do. Easy to say, but we don't just say it, we have measures in place because as the adage has it 'what is measured is done'. That helps in focusing our attention to the bits that don't work and to celebrate the bits that do, which in both cases show our colleagues how we define quality in the charity.

This work helps to continually shape and reshape the work that is going on in the charity. We have said repeatedly that the world continues to turn and in a changing world we can't continue to do what we did last year and expect it will continue to be effective. It helps ensure that the charity is in the best shape to deliver on its purpose, its 'fitness for intended use' if you like.

The philosophy of quality is closely aligned with this and for SJOG we're focused on:

- Outcomes for the people we support
- The flourishing of our colleagues
- Data-driven decision making
- Continuous improvement

The drivers of this philosophy are rooted in Deming and they inform our strategy, service models, policies and procedures, and training.

Each of the policies and statements that we have on our websites are all promises about the way we do things round here and create the expectations of people both within and outwith the charity.

What are your customers' expectations?

If we take Deming's point that the customer definition of quality is the only one that matters, then you need to understand what expectations they have of you, but first you need to understand who your customers are.

As an organisation you will have a whole host of customers, from the people that your charity serves, to funders, donors, colleagues, volunteers, wider family members and others. They will be specific to your charity.

We started with a stakeholder map that put the most important people closer to the centre and then those who are more distant customers at the end. The stakeholder map is segmented into sections to help focus on the areas that impact on your organisation.

You can use the handy radar below to signify the importance of the customer to your organisation.

Fig 15. Stakeholder mapping

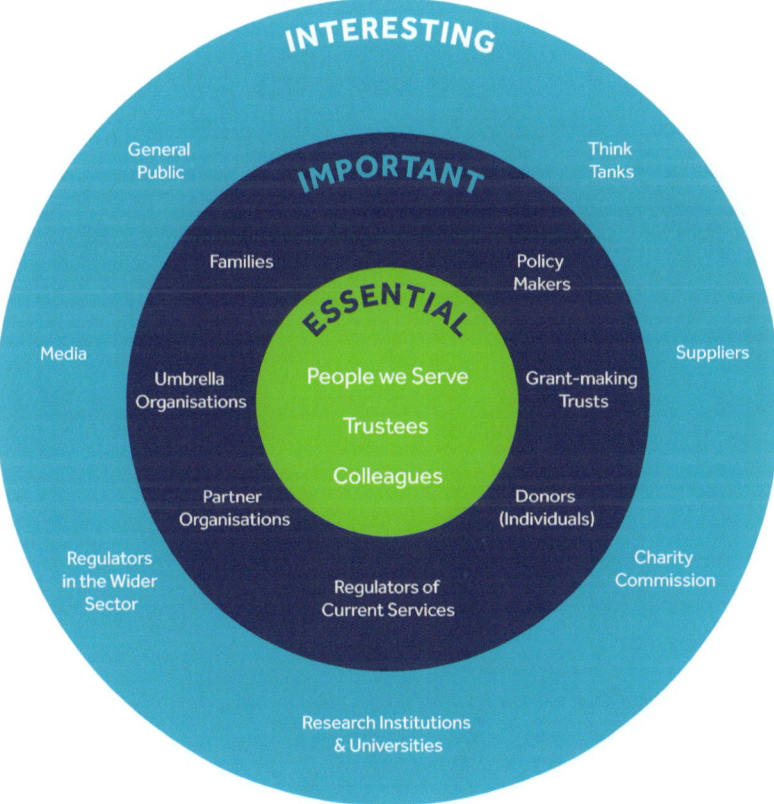

Having worked out who the most important customers are to you, the best way to work out what expectations they have of you is to ask them. Revolutionary I know, but people will mostly be happy to tell you what they like and what they are not so keen on about your organisation.

Just remember these are keyholes of truth and you'll need a range of views to build a sense of the gestalt.

Applying Deming's model, it is important that people are involved, have a voice in their service and the direction in which you are going. By adopting this philosophy means that quality is shaped around the 'person' and 'people'.

To adopt your philosophy you need to create your quality vision. Consider the following areas:

Fig 16. Engagement Planning

All these conversations generate a lot of information and a means for sorting through to the motifs, the repeating themes can be achieved through thematic analysis.

These conversations will also help you to predict and prepare for future challenges and have strategies in place to deal with these. Remember quality is about being in the right shape to best deliver on your purpose. You need to resist reacting with short term solutions; your focus needs to be on the long-term quality vision.

Simple truths, succinctly put

In an organisation you may have a single person leading on quality; that's ok as long as you know that no one person can deliver on quality. It requires everyone across your organisation to understand what is needed, and to deliver on this. This starts by being able to explain this to your colleagues in such a way that you make it easy for them to engage with.

Thematic analysis will take you so far. The challenge though is in further distilling these key thoughts into a form that your colleagues can hold on to, much like Tom Peters creating the McKinsey 7S model from the initial analysis.

Seek an aphorism. An aphorism is a truth succinctly put (and the thing that I like about this definition of aphorism is that it's an aphorism in its own right), and then communicate that truth like 'We're here to help', often.

In every organisation you'll have colleagues who will engage with change, those who will join given a little time and encouragement, and you'll have your 'no-no the penguins' (See 'Our Iceberg is melting').

The key point here is that you set the standards within your organisation. You choose what will celebrated, what will be tolerated and what will be challenged.

We support our colleagues but we also challenge them when the way they are acting or the standard of their work falls below what we deem as acceptable.

We've said that we need all of our colleagues to fulfil their responsibilities so that we can best deliver on the purpose of the charity. We're looking for all of our colleagues to engage with the good work that we do and do it to a high standard. We support them to do this through the development of a quality policy and a quality plan.

Creating good quality habits

We like a policy in SJOG. It's a promise to our colleagues about how we will deal with things, and it sets the standard. When rolling out a policy we need to consider the audience who will receive the information. The policy needs to be kept as simple as possible but no simpler, which is a skill in itself.

At the beginning of the chapter, I talked about engagement and collaboration. This is the golden thread, and the tone and structure of the policy should be written in a style that is as easy for our colleagues to engage with and share.

It's worth highlighting that the approach taken is in alignment with the ISO9001 seven quality principles.

Fig 17. ISO 9001 Quality principles

> **QMP 1 - Customer focus: Meeting** - and exceeding - your customers current and future needs is the primary focus of quality management.
>
> **QMP 2 - Readership**: Having a unified direction and mission that comes from strong leadership is essential in promoting the right culture.
>
> **QMP 3 - Engagement of people:** Competent, empowered and engaged people at all levels of your organisation.
>
> **QMP 4 - Process approach:** Understanding activities as processes that link together and function as a system to yeild more effective and efficient results.
>
> **QMP 5 - Improvement:** Successful organisations have an ongoing improvement focus.
>
> **QMP 6 - Evidence-based decision-making:** Ensuring your decisions are based on the analysis and evaluation of data is more likely to produce the desired result.
>
> **QMP 7 - Relationship management:** Identifying the important relationships you have with interested parties such as your suppliers - and setting out a plan to manage them - will drive sustained success.

Your quality plan should never be solely the responsibility of one person. I say the more the merrier. You should already know by now who your interested parties are, because you highlighted them in your customer mapping, so involve them as much as possible.

Some interested parties may not be involved in the day to day responsibility of managing your organisation. Rather, they are impacted by quality and therefore have an important stake in the successful outcome of your quality plan e.g. people you provide services to or their families etc. It's worth spending some time thinking about this and adding to your customer mapping to identify:

- Who?
- Internal or external?
- Needs and expectations?
- How will we meet these?
- Who is responsible?

Creating your quality plan should be relatively straight forward once you have listened to people. Where the challenge lies is in the ever changing and complex world that we all live in. The world continues to turn so focus on the long term quality rather than just the challenges of today.

Questions to ask yourself

- Have you considered if your quality initiatives are the right ones?
- Are they truly aligned with your business plan?

Quality framework - bringing it all together

> "Quality is the result of a carefully constructed cultural environment. It has to be the fabric of the organisation', not part of the fabric."
>
> Phil Crosby

There's a project management triangle that shows the interplay of the factors that affect the quality of what you provide:

Fig 18. The Project Management Triangle

In the delivery of a project, if you want it delivered more quickly, you'll either need to invest in extra resources (people, technology) or reduce the scope of the final project if you want to maintain the same quality. Time is a factor and if you are not convinced by that last statement, then try drawing a portrait of yourself in 10 minutes, 10 seconds and 1 second – which comes closer to looking human?

To give you a scenario:

We provide services to people. In a service we provide 24-hour support to a group of people living together. We normally have three people on shift throughout the week, but on a Monday, Joan phones in with flu and states they will be out all week. That impacts on the rota and reduces the resources that we have in the service.

We can't provide less than 24-hour support, even though we have reduced resources. So how do we manage this?

The answer lies in Scope, Time and Resources.

The options are:

1. Reduce the time, in this case the number of hours of support provided by working with a person down, so that the current team has to work a bit harder and a bit faster to get all of the tasks done.

2. You could reduce the scope by cutting some of the tasks that the reduced team has to do, like spending less one-to-one time with the people being supported.

3. You could cover the shifts by asking colleagues to work overtime, or bringing in bank staff and agency staff, effectively adding more resources to make sure that the time and quality remain the same.

Time, scope and resources. That's your choice. Even if you said bring in more technology and reduce the need for people, that's investing in resource to reduce time. Inextricably linked.

Now if we take that scenario a step further and on the Tuesday, Jaspreet and Joe also phone in with the flu. Then the decisions we make might be different because there are different quality requirements; we have a legal requirement to run a safe service; we have standards that our regulator sets and then we have our internal quality standards as well, but in each case the decision is time, resource or scope.

For us our internal standards are higher than either our legal or regulatory requirements because we believe that as a charity where people support people what we do is important, and that we should always be striving to offer better help to the people that we are here to serve.

So how do we know that we are good?

Simply, we measure it. We have a series of quality statements about the way that we do things. We've written this down and shared it widely; we have a plan about how we will get better, and we have worked to get the buy in of our colleagues, and all of this is wrapped up in our quality framework that has quality assurance built into it.

We have decided what we will measure in the charity and we collect that information. Some of this information is collected automatically as our colleagues use technology in their daily roles. Some of it is more nuanced and requires quality audits by our colleagues and the people that we support.

Lisa, our chief operating officer, calls all of the systems that we have in place, our quality framework, which she describes as:

"the identification and subsequent elimination of issues through meaningful reporting and effective decision-making."

As we covered in the purpose chapter, good information about what is going on in your charity is vital, whether that's the keyholes of truth, or the data on the trustees dashboard.

Good information helps our operational colleagues gain clarity about what's going on in the charity right now and where potential issues are arising, and which parts of the charity are flying. Trend analysis helps with targeting further improvement.

What's most important for our regulators is that we can evidence excellent practice. Previously it existed but without the ability to evidence the quality of our colleagues' work, we couldn't share it with others, celebrate it or even include it in our quality ratings.

These days our quality framework is the 'go to' place to strengthen your resolve and avoid costly scenarios such as letting quality standards drop, or during busy periods, cutting back on quality checks. If you don't have quality frameworks in place then you will not have a controlled environment with a consistent approach to quality right down to a granular level.

Deming termed quality as 'everyone's responsibility' therefore the framework needs to touch and influence everyone in the organisation. It is important that colleagues understand and are aware of this.

At SJOG, we build this into our induction programme where we set the expectations and then this is restated in our meetings, supervisions, annual performance reviews, continuous professional development, and we report on this annually at SJOG staff conferences.

Now we love a number and a chart in SJOG. Understanding the data indicators (or expected standards) are important and are influenced by everyone in the organisation, but whilst numbers are useful, it's much more powerful to support this by telling stories. Stories are the best way to communicate the impact and outcome of what we do and celebrate good work.

Professor Don Berwick, who is an advisor to the Kings Fund Think Tank highlighted that organisations need a clear ambition and plan for improvement. To do this successfully requires good reliable information about what is happening. He believed, as do I, that the strongest information comes from the narrative - it's the stories about what has gone well and what hasn't that people hold onto and helps them both to understand 'this is what good looks like' and to see the meaningful contribution they are making in people's lives. This is where real quality improvements happen.

Your quality framework should support your management reporting systems and help centralise data information. Trending issues will be exposed and assist in predicting what you may need to do in the future or what to escalate immediately. The framework will assist colleagues in reflecting and evaluating certain situations or events, through reliable data information and thus develop a climate and culture of quality overall.

Questions to ask yourself

- Do you have a structured process in place to meet your quality expectations?
- Do you have internal data standards e.g. key performance indicators that you measure?
- Do you identify and analyse causes of excellence as well as problems?
- Does your framework centralise data to make it easier to analyse?

Putting theory into practice

The situation and brief

In December 2018, SJOG had 26 services across the UK ranging from provision for older communities to people with learning and physical disabilities, and mental health issues. Fifteen of these were regulated by the Care Quality Commission (CQC). Our services for people experiencing homelessness, modern day slavery and our day opportunities didn't fall within the CQC remit and appeared to sit outside of any quality procedures.

Services did not work in unity due to divisive structures. The quality assurance policy and procedure were neither consistent nor up to date. Quality was poorly defined and lacked clarity in job roles and quality was someone else's responsibility.

The Care Quality Commission (CQC) rated a third of the services that they regulated as 'requiring improvement' in at least one area.

Occupancy levels in our services appeared to be unmanaged and the figures that we did have were unreliable. There was a training offer, but this had just had seven mandatory courses on offer to colleagues.

Services were in decline and commissioning teams were unhappy due to a lack of quality and outcomes for people. SJOG had previously provided 47 services but by 2018 had declined to 26, two of which were under threat of being transferred to other providers towards the end of 2018.

A previous restructure had not been fully implemented and the residual effect was still clear to see - the word 'raw' comes to mind.

Some operational managers maintained that quality was very high, and others were brave enough to say there was a problem. There were four camps in the operational team and none of which came together to discuss quality, share good practices and learn when things went wrong. Tensions were high and lots of spinning plates were falling quickly. The brief was about making sense of this and stabilising the situation quickly whilst having an eye to the long-term sustainability of services.

What is 'really' going on?

To understand the reality of quality in our charity, we needed to get out there! Sometimes we organised visits and other times we just showed up. Of course, this needs to be balanced and consented to when it is someone's own home, but even that dialogue of planning and the willingness or otherwise of colleagues, are in themselves a rich source of information.

I call these a 'service health check', and these are really important especially as a new leader coming into a well-established organisation. It helps to develop relationships and conversation with people accessing services and with colleagues. These visits are informal, relaxed and sociable occasions. They are useful in breaking down the 'them and us' perception. The more engagement the better - this helps to establish collaboration and eliminates fear of change.

There are no set criteria for a service health check but my advice is not to make it overly complicated and formal as it puts people off. It is vital that you don't go in just looking at systems and processes as this will come across like an inspection. Get a feeling for people, who they are, how they live, how they work etc.

You also may want to do a bit of homework before arriving. For example:

- Read reports e.g. CQC inspection reports.
- Check the financial viability of the service.
- What is the void situation?
- What is the recruitment situation? Is agency being used?
- Read management reports-check all levels from first line management upwards.
- Satisfaction surveys.
- Is the service meeting their performance targets?
- Any risk factors e.g. safeguardings, disciplinary and grievance matters. These help to understand the practices (and habits) in the organisation and also the sub-cultures that may be evident.

The hard data described above helps evaluation of the local, regional and national context. I always encourage my colleagues to question all data, challenge it and test it. It tells us a useful story about quality.

So, what did we find?

The final part of this chapter is the outcomes from this story. Outcomes are what draw people in, and seeing the improvements helps our colleagues see that their work is meaningful and so they invest more of their time in helping to achieve more outcomes.

Organisational Impact:

- Reputational damage e.g. contractual requirements not being fulfilled and at risk.

Social care operations related:

Between January and March 2019 the service health checks were fully completed and the data alongside the narrative told the real story of what was going on:

- CQC ratings were: Safe (87%), Caring (100%), Effective (80%), Responsive (93%) and Well Led (80%).
- These ratings were flattering as there had been a decline in quality since services' last CQC inspection. A quality scoring system based on the Key Lines of Enquiry (KLOE) was developed and 80% of services were rated either 'requires improvement' or 'inadequate'.
- Some operational managers complained that quality was not their responsibility and tried to resist a new quality approach.
- Mandatory training on average was poor across all services, including those that were not regulated.
- Management reporting was ineffective and lacked drive and direction of action.
- There were 168 policies, most of which were out of date and overly complicated. There were too many policies, which were dated in terminology, contradictory and not consistent with modern day social care practices.
- There was a fear of failure and blame was a common theme across all services.
- No autonomy at a service level with all decisions expected to go through leaders.
- No relationship with commissioners.
- No reviews of fees had taken place for many years. In some cases, over a decade.
- No action taken against voids, yet staffing levels remained the same.
- No awareness of the reality of the situation.
- We identified the hot spots and focused on these services immediately.

Average quality performance was rated at 34%

What came next?

It wasn't always smooth sailing. Relationships with commissioners in one authority were damaged by a historical dispute over whether the charity had delivered on a contract and we couldn't provide the evidence to say it had been. There were redundancy processes, we were practically insolvent and when we established how many people we were supporting, it was 25% less than the charity believed it was supporting.

The key message here is when things are difficult, focus on the quality vision and the long-term plan. We prioritised starting with areas that caused safety concerns, then legal concerns, then regulatory concerns, but we created learning forums sharing the learning with colleagues and commissioners on what we had identified and most important the actions that were in place to rectify this.

We evidenced everything that we did by creating our own quality dashboards and centralised quality risk register. Our 'KLOE Cloud' as I call it was created for every service.

Quality outcomes

Within three months we had seen improvement but there was much more work to do. We tracked quality performance every day and reported this monthly. We provided managers with their quality scores and helped them to develop by using a 'Plan, Do, Check, Act' approach.

By the end of 2019:

- Average CQC ratings were: Safe (87%), Caring (100%), Effective (87%), Responsive (93%) and Well Led (87%). This was based on recent CQC inspections.
- Quality outcomes indicated 100% services were sustaining good quality.
- New mandatory induction process was introduced for all colleagues.
- Learning pathways were developed for each role in the organisation.
- We increased our Learning & Development offer from 7 to 60 courses ranging in mandatory and specialist courses.

- All contracts were stable, and we opened 5 new services.
- Policies were reduced from 168 to 51 and all aligned to quality with lead authors.

Average quality performance was rated at 68%.

By the end of 2020:

- Average CQC ratings were: Safe (93%), Caring (100%), Effective (93%), Responsive (100%) and Well Led (100%). This was based on recent CQC inspections. Remaining services were yet to be inspected.
- 1 service was Outstanding and 2 had outstanding features in Responsive and Effective.
- Occupancy averaged 94%, which was achieved during the covid pandemic.
- We added a further 30 courses in management and leadership.
- A leadership and management competency framework was aligned to quality assurance.
- We opened 10 further services. 2 services were also re-modelled to develop more specialist provision.
- The charity was awarded its first tenders in 17 years, awarded in 2 local authorities.

Average quality performance was rated at 89%

By 2022:

- There are now 52 services.
- 100% of services are rated as Good or Outstanding by our regulators.
- Infection control audits by CCGs and/or local authorities averaging at 96%.
- Developed a new Learning & Development Plan for aspiring, developing and outstanding managers. This added another 10 courses, totalling 142 courses.

- Refreshed workshop on quality assurance and also performance management to avoid any complacency.

Average quality performance was rated at 94%

Colleagues can now see that the steps that we take improve quality of life outcomes for the people we are here to support. Deming captured this well:

> "There is no route to excellence other than the joy and work. You can't exhort, beat, incentivise a workforce to achieve excellence. You can achieve compliance but not excellence."

We are starting to see the evidence of excellence albeit three years on. Our learning would be that there are no quick fixes with quality. It requires keeping your eye firmly focused on the long-term vision of what your services could be and then taking steps towards that.

For us it's meant that new colleagues joining the organisation come into an organisation with an established standard to the way that we do things around here, and we expect them to be at least this good. Quality builds quality.

Complacency is the enemy of success

It's often stated that Aristotle said, 'Quality is an act not a habit'.

But what does this mean in terms of leading on quality? Well, it's all about the habits that we create and is what drives any organisation. From what we deliver to and for people, to processes, and resources to the entire workforce.

Quality is a big deal and needs to be taken seriously as it decides the success or failure of any organisation.

There are lots of definitions of 'quality', dependent upon which community of practice or discipline you work in, but we focus on the quality of life for the people that we are here to serve; effectively are we fulfilling our purpose?

Our funders come to us because we do what we say, and we can show them that we spend their money in a way that positively impacts on a person's life.

The biggest move in the charity has been away from having to dig to uncover pockets of excellent practice, to having demonstrable quality across all of our services.

Whatever your preferred definition, quality does need to be a habit. We all know there are good and bad habits, both of which become a behaviour, which then form a culture. Quality is not just about processes and procedures, it's also about setting an expectation which therefore helps to shape a culture, and it's that culture that resists complacency, and it does need constant attention.

There were many challenges in the charity's approach to quality that needed a myriad of approaches, with a number of colleagues undertaking different parts of the system to achieve the common goal of quality. Jim Collins' book 'Good and Great' termed this the Flywheel Effect:

> "No matter how dramatic the end result, good-to-great transformations never happen in one fell swoop. In building a great company or social sector enterprise, there is no single defining action, no grand program, no one killer innovation, no solitary lucky break, no miracle moment. Rather, the process resembles relentlessly pushing a giant, heavy flywheel, turn upon turn, building momentum until a point of breakthrough, and beyond."

As a leader you have a responsibility to create habits and set the expectations, by creating an environment that colleagues can continue to improve what we do and how we do it.

As a leader I am acutely aware that I need to walk the walk, but more importantly leave a good pathway for others to follow, and hopefully improve.

Collins makes a really good point that we need to be relentless. Setting a vision for the team so that everyone understands the common goal was essential. Every colleague had a part to play. Sweating the small stuff was just as important as the bigger elements of quality, so distributing leadership so that everyone took responsibility was important. This means that we were distracted about the right things, by the right people in the right roles.

The flywheel helped to create the culture of 'quality as a habit' and whilst breakthroughs came thick and fast (and also a few curve balls), we had our eyes firmly on the future to achieve excellence.

> "Excellence is never an accident. It is always the result of high intention, sincere effort, and intelligent execution; it represents the wise choice of many alternatives - choice, not chance, and determines your destiny."
>
> Aristotle

Reflection
Change programmes work best when you are clear about what will need resolving and supporting to get through these.

References

Chartered Quality institute (2022) What is Quality https://www.quality.org/what-quality.

University of Tennessee (2022) Demings 14 Points https://www.uthsc.edu/its/business-productivity-solutions/lean-uthsc/deming.php

150 9001 (2022) What are the principles of1509001 seen at https://www.iso-9001-checklist.co.uk/what-are-the-principles-of-150- 9001.htm

Collins, J. (2001).Good to Great: Why Some Companies Make the Leap ...and Others Don't. London: Random House.

Aristotle cited in Te'o, T.. The Pursuit of Service Excellence: how business intelligence can drive service improvement. In Australian Network University Planners Conference (ANUP 2019). University of Southern Queensland.

A successful future

Building in innovation and opportunities from the very beginning

What you will find here:

- An overview of innovation and some of the challenges in communicating it
- A description of what you need to start to embed a culture of innovation
- Approaches to help you generate new ideas

Introduction

Innovation is everywhere. Organisations include the term innovation in their vision, mission, and objective statements. Politicians regularly mention the term innovation in speeches (Kahn, 2018). Everyone reading this book will have heard of it, even if they are not entirely sure why it's in this book.

In this chapter we move beyond the word of innovation. We provide a description of setting the context that provides a chance for innovative ideas and services to emerge that respond to the needs of the people we serve. To do so the culture of the organisation needs certain structures and part of this is achieved through embedding a consistent methodology aimed at nurturing innovation.

We've called the chapter 'A Successful Future' and focus on both opportunities and innovation deliberately. We define the reason a little later but opportunities reflect the approach needed to create new services (or approaches), embrace them, take advantage of them, and sometimes say no to them in order to meaningfully guide a charity into growth and in response to changing policy and economic landscapes.

We provide practical examples of our experience of setting up an opportunities team. Not everything has been a success so we will give examples of where these have and have not worked.

Innovation is everywhere but what is it?

O'Brian (2013) reported that the word innovation was the most over-used word in America but that many organisations still find innovation elusive.

Kahn (2018) says this is because there is a misunderstanding that innovation is focused on creating something completely new.

However, innovation isn't just about delivering radical new products or services but also about incremental improvement.

In a recent article in the Harvard Business Review, Nadya Zhexembayeva refreshingly wrote about the need to stop calling 'it' 'innovation'. Referring to recent research, she argues that people react negatively to the word innovation. For some innovation seems corporate, profit driven and means additional work above and beyond the day to day job. Zhexembayeva comments that using other terms help people engage more with the process.

This is important as innovation is both an outcome and a process, and it requires a method to focuses on solving problems and deliver an outcome.

There is a lot here. So below we unpick this. We start with a definition and progress with the importance of mindset, process and outcomes.

A definition of innovation

There is much writing on the definition of innovation. Here is one as an example:

> "...[innovation is a] multi-stage process whereby organisation transform ideas into new/improved products, services or processes, in order to advance, compete and differentiate themselves successfully in their marketplace."
>
> Baregheh et al, 2009

What all definitions have in common is a recognition that innovation is a multi-stage process in order to reach a new status (e.g. product, service or system). It is not achieved through a one-off meeting. It is through consistent work following a process that takes place across an extended period of time.

This process, Tim Brown CEO of design consultancy IDEO defines as 'nonlinear', which is a nice way of recognising that it takes a fair bit of trial and error. Failure is a key part of the process when trying new ideas, as is learning from this and iterating improvements.

Innovation isn't just about research and development in new commercial products. The term social innovation has been used to describe the work of not-for-profits. Stanford Business School define social innovation as:

> "The process of developing and deploying effective solutions to challenging and often systemic social and environmental issues in support of social progress."

A good example here is IDEO.org. They are a design studio based in the USA which focuses on innovation to address a variety of social problems. Their work has ranged from designing portable lighting for areas with little or no electricity through to the development of tools that open conversations about family planning and contraception for young women in Ethiopia.

What underpins their work is the multi-stage nonlinear process which helps understand different contexts and situations in detail and then finds space for new services or ways of offering support.

> **Top tip:**
> There are plenty of off the shelf toolkits which support innovation processes. A list to get you started is at the end of this chapter.

Mindset

A mindset is a set of attitudes, values and beliefs that affect the way you act. People have a mindset but so do groups of people, and this includes organisations.

Not all individuals or organisations have an innovation mindset. It doesn't mean this can't be developed, just that it will need a bit of leadership.

Encompassing a mindset that predisposes individuals and organisations to be risk-taking, cross-disciplinary, and open to varied ways of thinking helps to establish the state necessary for innovation; state implies something habitual and lasting (Kahn, 2018).

Dyer, Gregerson and Christensen (2011) looking across organisations known for innovation found five skills that push new ways of thinking, spur and support innovation:

1. Associating is drawing connections between questions, problems, or ideas from unrelated fields;
2. Questioning is posing queries that challenge common wisdom;
3. Observing is scrutinising the behaviour of customers, suppliers and competitors to identify new ways of doing things;
4. Experimenting is constructing interactive experiences and provoking unorthodox responses to see what insights emerge; and
5. Networking is meeting people with different ideas and perspectives.

These five skills prepare and enable organisations to think differently, laterally, and expansively.

The other trait that is required is one unhindered by failure (Luchs, 2016). In innovation, success is desirable but not guaranteed and the iterative processes demand learning from failures. Having colleagues and senior teams in charities comfortable with this approach is important. Failure is a real possibility.

We introduced the idea that the term innovation can be a bit of a blocker in getting people involved so we'll use the term 'opportunities' from now on and explain a little of why that is.

What we did at SJOG

SJOG was in a bit of pickle, but no matter how much of hole you are in, you always need to build towards something and that requires a future focus.

The world will continue to turn and organisations, even charities, must be prepared to meet it as it does.

In 2018, SJOG decided to advertise for a 'Director of Opportunities', who would sit as part of the senior team. The role was new to the organisation and in a time of crisis the case had to be made that the role was important enough to direct much needed funds to this.

The argument was that this role was not to focus on what we did today but what we would need to do tomorrow to be of more help to more people.

This wasn't about doing more of the kind of work that we already did, but entirely new ways of working.

The use of the term 'opportunities' was deliberate. The post was about carving out new opportunities for the organisation so that it could be of more help to more people - taking ideas through to implementation.

The phrase innovation would give the wrong connotations; the internal perception may have been a mystical process that would be difficult to engage with, particularly when the organisation was already going through a rapid period of change.

Put simply, 'opportunities' is easier to understand and engage with.

The ingredients

Once in post our director of opportunities had the job of embedding a process to develop new ideas and then taking those ideas through to implementation. Having a structured process is the ways and means of making innovation happen and seeing a tangible outcome. Process involves people, time and creativity.

People

It might sound obvious but there a need to invest in people with skills in innovation. Ed Catmull, founder of Pixar, says in his book Creativity Inc that he always used to ask audiences when speaking what was more important - good people or good ideas?

His belief was that if you give a good idea to a bad team they will mess it up. If you give a bad idea to a good team, they will improve on it or throw it out and find something better. In all of his time presenting this, he was only challenged once that ideas come from people.

If we go back to Tim Brown's definition of innovation as a nonlinear process (managed trial and error) it needs a group of people within the organisation who are comfortable with this.

Bring together a group of people who have different styles of problem solving, different skill sets, can bring a different perspective to a particular problem. This doesn't mean that everyone needs to have a qualification in 'innovation'.

Although there may be a core team responsible for leading on opportunities within an organisation, it is important that colleagues across the organisation are engaged. The people who deliver services and work to support people are fountains of knowledge. Using their wisdom and experience of operational delivery can help identify risks in new ideas and weed out any sticky points that might happen.

The link between the people focused on opportunities and the colleagues at the sharp end is fundamental to success. In SJOG the operations teams that deliver services are best placed to advise on the nitty gritty of ideas and how they might be delivered in practice. They are also the best people to tell you what doesn't work and what causes frustrations in the delivery of services. The open relationship, a focus on making things better through iteration and collaboration is central.

Engaging colleagues broadly has benefits. It helps expose people to new ways of working and gives them the permission to try and improve the things that don't work, or don't work as well as they could. It shows trust in our colleagues and shows that we respect their expertise.

It also builds the culture of innovation across the organisation.

On the face of it financially it does not cost any extra; it does require colleagues' time, and they will of course have a job to do. In SJOG, operational teams focus on delivering quality services 24/7. Their primary driver is to provide support to the people in front of them. Therefore, if they are also responsible for creating the new wave of services there is a danger it becomes a second thought.

This is where leadership is needed to commit time and resources to be able to support these initiatives.

Time

Doing something new, or finding a way to improve what you are currently doing takes time and energy, and there is no guarantee of success. In fact as we have stated, failure is not only a real possibility but part of the non-linear process.

However if you stand still doing the same things that you have always done there will become a point when you are as useful as a VHS recorder. Sure, some people still love them, but the rest of the world has moved on.

You will need to invest time to look at new ways of working and that requires a concerted effort to create space to think, and for colleagues from across the organisation to come together to work through the process of innovation

There are specific forums that can be used for this such as conferences, workshops and internal initiatives that use a specific method (this latter point is described a little later in the chapter).

In 2019 two conferences were held to bring colleagues together and start to shape a new future for SJOG. The first was in February 2019 which was an introduction to the new executive team where we shared the challenges the organisation faced, the good stuff that was happening and we started to focus on the future of SJOG.

The second was in September 2019 and specifically focused on new opportunities aligned to a new strategy and engaging 100 colleagues in an innovation process.

Conference - February 2019

In this conference, we ran a 45-minute session looking at what opportunities existed for SJOG. It focused on what do we do now and what can we do in the future. Opportunity charts were developed (see figure 19) which focused on the different areas of support SJOG provide.

By doing this, it was possible to consider where there was space for innovation and use this to discover the area in more detail. The tool was used as a discussion prompt.

Fig 19. Opportunity chart to identify areas of work to 'discover', denoted in green.

AREA	AIM	CURRENT METHOD	NEW (additional method)	NEW (additional method)	NEW (additional method)	NEW (additional method)
1 Community	Community-based projects that give people the chance to have fun, learn and grow	Digswell Community Gardening Project Outreach activities in Enfield	Service to support younger generation - vulnerable young people and people who are disengaged	Transition services supporting younger people	Support for ex-offenders	Services focused on rural inclusions
2 Housing/Health	We provide residential care homes shaped to meet the needs of the people living in them, both in physical adaptations and in the care and support that is offered	Variety of residential care settings supporting people with challenging needs, profound physical disabilities and learning disabilities	Dementia support	Crisis bed following hospital treatment	Mental health support	Places for those under 16 years old
3 Housing Supported Living	We support people to live how and where they choose and with the right care and support	Domiciliary care in north and south of the country Supporting people with physical and learning disabilities	Those who need more complex support such as nursing needs	Mental health support	Young people	People affected by domestic abuse

This was the first time colleagues had been engaged in this way. The output was useful to an extent e.g. identifying transition services for young people with autism, but of more benefit was that it broke the ice, that we could do something new, and introduced the concept of innovation to our colleagues at SJOG.

Conference - September 2019

Later in the year we ran a further innovation session with 100 colleagues.

The focus of this conference was on how we could generate ideas that could make SJOG bigger, bolder or brighter. Bigger was about where opportunities aligned for us to do more of what we already did.

Bolder was about finding new ways of delivering on our purpose.

Brighter was about finding better ways to do what we did now, whether that was changing the purchase order system, or how we did our care planning.

We worked with innovation experts Freestyle Innovation who offered pro bono support to facilitate the session.

We constructed a day-long programme of work that helped colleagues generate ideas that were focused around realising the new strategy that

SJOG had produced. The workshop was split into several interactive sessions:

Fig 20. Questions to frame thinking around SJOG's strategy.

1 How might we be of more benefit to more people?

Starter for 10 ideas
This is about the people we support.

- What could you do differently to improve our quality?
- Could you explore new areas of work? What would the be?
- How might you better meet the needs of the people we support? Is technology an answer?

2. How might better support our colleagues?

Starter for 10 ideas
This is about how each of us support each other in the organisation:

- How might we make better care of the people who work and volunteer for us?
- How should/could you be rewarded?
- How might we be more attractive employer for you and others especially those over 50?

3 How might we grow as a charity?

Starter for 10 ideas
This is about how me grow and what we do next:

- What could we do that we don't do now? What now would you play?
- What other areas of work do you think we should explore?
- What do you think we do really well? How could we do more of it?

4 How might we become more sustainable?

Starter for 10 ideas
This is about how we make sure we can be here for a long time and how we can do our bit for the world around us

- Could you be more efficient at work?
- Could you care for the environment better? How should we support this?

- How might we? Four key questions were asked relating the new strategy and how we might move to realise it. These are shown in Figure 20. This was to encourage our colleagues to think about these areas before they arrived so that it wasn't a complete surprise as to the focus of the work. Working in groups of 10 people any idea generated was listed on a post-it note.

- Opportunity area. From the ideas created (the opportunities) the task then focused on selecting an idea to focus on, work up and iterate in the rest of the workshop.

- The big idea. After selecting an idea, groups worked this up using notes, drawings and prompts. Questions were used to direct the discussions and help creativity. At lunch each idea was displayed so everyone in the workshop could vote and make notes on them. This allowed broader engagement with ideas and aimed to generate divergent thinking across our colleagues as they saw ideas that others had posed.

- The big golden idea. Using the feedback from the notes made, each idea was worked up using an A4 promotional style page and submitted. We then talked about some of these at the end of the conference.

There are many methods that can be used to run workshops like this, but doing so paves a way to start the innovation process and also shows that all colleagues have a part to play. Importantly, it shows that the organisation is making the time to engage in the process and that it is acceptable for everyone to have a part in it.

The day was full of energy and identified a number of initiatives, but most importantly it showed our colleagues that they could use their creativity to make things better.

> **Questions to ask yourself**
> - What simple question(s) would help me understand the needs of the people our charity serves?
> - What can we measure which help us to understand the difference we make?
> - What resources do we need to answer the two questions above?
> - How can you create space and time for innovation in your work?

Creativity

Brothers Tom and David Kelly, founders of IDEO, talk about reclaiming creativity:

> "Most people are born creative. As children, we revel in imaginary play, ask outlandish questions, draw blobs and call them dinosaurs. But over time, because of socialisation and formal education, a lot of us start to stifle those impulses. We learn to be warier of judgment, more cautious, more analytical. The world seems to divide into 'creatives' and 'non-creatives', and too many people consciously or unconsciously resign themselves to the latter category."

In the introduction we detailed that innovation can be a radical big bang, but that it can also be an incremental change.

In SJOG the focus of the opportunities team is to create something that is new and not merely an iteration of what a charity already does. Creativity is needed in order to do something different and ensure outcomes moves beyond what would be a natural development.

We are born creative but it's also something that we need to practise (Kelly & Kelly 2012) and, as described, investment in people and time is needed. The challenge for charities is to embrace the creativity we all have and form an environment that is supportive towards creative problem solving that drives innovation.

A consistent method needs to be applied to make colleagues comfortable with the messy unknown and fear of failure that this brings. Design thinking is an approach which uses tools and techniques that maximise creativity to solve a particularly problem.

Design thinking is using the approach that is used to design new products. It's about a process that takes an idea through to implementation, and it is a disciplined process. Just to be clear on that design is a discipline, but it thrives on creativity.

In 2008, Tim Brown wrote that design thinking is a methodology that focuses on innovation in response to the observations of what people want or need in their lives, what they like or dislike and using these insights to form a solution. What we mean here is that by observing the specific needs of the people that you are here to support, identification of new ways to support them emerge, but remember it is not a nice linear process but an iterative process.

Hilary Cottam was recognised as the UK Designer of the Year in 2005 for applying the design approach to social issues such as prisoner re-offending rates. Her book Radical Help shows the benefit the approach can have and the importance of understanding the problem in detail rather than jumping to a solution. In the examples of her work she defines relationships as a major catalyst to addressing social needs. Most importantly though, through observing people their needs are fully understood.

At SJOG we start with need.

Fridays for the future

We talked earlier about engagement through conferences. This works at one level but large groups can't work in detail through the design thinking methodology over the course of a few hours.

SJOG created an initiative called Fridays for the Future where a group comes together to explore a particular problem (and opportunity).

Design thinking processes are used so that ideas are ready to be put forward for funding. The initiative is at an early stage but provides a means for creating an internal multi-disciplinary group to drive forward opportunities at SJOG.

Innovation process

So, having spoken about design thinking, how do you go about putting it into practice? Design thinking is a process with tools that can be applied to each stage.

The UK's Design Council is a useful resource for this. Figure 21 depicts perhaps the most common and well-known depiction of design thinking- the double diamond approach. Adhering to this approach (others are available!) offers a way to manage risk and offers a structured process for everyone to engage with.

Essentially there are two steps and the two diamonds present the process of exploring a particular issue or challenge deeply (diamond 1) and then taking focused action (diamond 2) to deliver the solution to the issue or challenge.

Fig 21. The Double Diamond approach to design thinking. Adapted from the Design Council, 2019

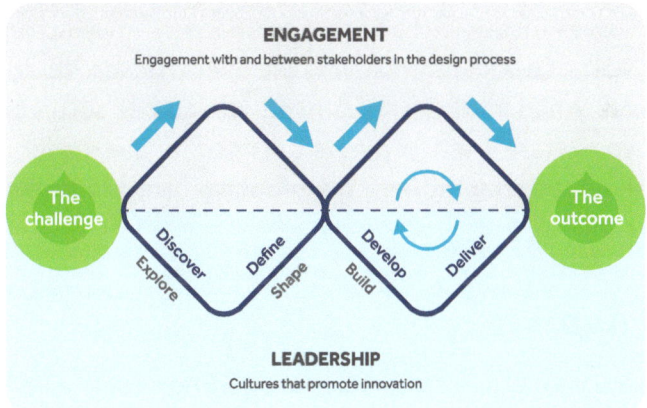

Each diamond has two focused activities, which need to be followed in order to get the maximum from the process.

The first diamond helps people **Discover** and understand, rather than simply assume, what the problem is. It involves speaking to and spending time with people who are affected by the issue(s). This is important. The whole process is problem focused rather than solution focused.

Although technology can be an attractive solution, it might not be one that is fit for purpose. Take time to observe, interview, run workshops and ask honest questions. This part of the process shouldn't be rushed as this will help make sure you are delivering a solution that addresses the needs of the people the charity is here to support.

Once complete you should start to **Define** the challenge in a different way. This involves analysing all the information you have gathered, looking for common themes and trends and defining the problem you are trying to solve, or the need you are meeting. This will form the anchor point for the solutions that follow.

We then move on to the second triangle and **Develop**. This is where you should focus on giving different answers to the clearly defined problem, seeking inspiration from elsewhere and co-designing with the people you support, colleagues who support them and where needed, external stakeholders. The beauty of design thinking is that you shouldn't settle on the first solution that emerged. Be comfortable with scrapping an idea and starting again if needed.

Delivery involves testing out different solutions at small-scale, rejecting those that will not work and improving the ones that will. Iteration should be embraced. When writing a document, you do not settle on the first produced, you iterate it until it meets the need for the reader. The same approach should be adopted here, go through prototyping at a small scale where you can.

REACH App.

At SJOG we run an outreach services supporting people who have been subject to modern day slavery. It was proposed that some of the support sessions could be supported through using tablets and MS Teams. In practice this didn't happen.

The people we support didn't have the digital skills to access MS teams and preferred using mobiles to communicate. This prompted us to rethink this and about how we can offer support in a way that better addresses the needs of this multi-national community.

We came up with the concept for a mobile app that would provide resources and self-help to the people we support. Importantly it would do this in a language of their choice - one of the biggest problems we identified.

To develop this, we carried out wireframing prototypes - wireframes of paper models of the different parts of a digital system (e.g. a phone screen or pages on a website). We mocked these up on the computer, printed them and ran a focus group to get feedback (see figure 22). The benefit of this was that we could tease out simple issues without the expense of a full system.

Being on paper also made the participants more willing to engage - it's much easier to write on a piece of paper than critique something on a screen! We'd encourage you to use simple prototyping methods like this.

Fig 22. Reach App wireframe development

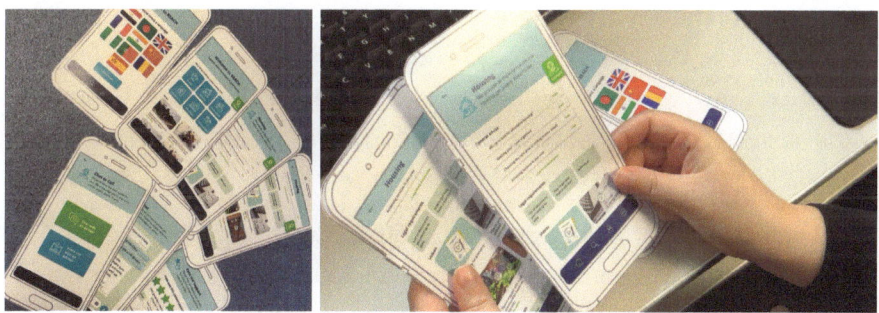

Wireframing is one method that can be useful. Other methods include:

- Generating personas which are fictional descriptions of people who you might be designing for. Importantly these are realistic rather than idealistic.

- The SCAMPER technique for creative thinking. SCAMPER is an acronym for: Substitute, Combine, Adapt, Modify, Put to another use, Eliminate, Reverse.

- To use SCAMPER as a group, you take an existing service and work through each area above. For example, what happens if you put the service to another use by supporting a different group of people). Doing this helps broaden thinking and can help identify new ways to address need.

There are lots of tools and at the end of the chapter we've listed some useful reading on this.

> ## Questions to ask yourself
> - When have we tested an idea before implementation?
> - Could we pilot more ideas and get feedback using some of the methods described above?

Sounds good, does it work?

The takeaway message regarding design thinking is that it is very much focused on understanding the problem in as much detail as possible. To do this, particularly in the charity sector, where we exist for public benefit, is to understand the people you are supporting in as much detail as possible, and the best way to do this is to include them in the process. Using this person-centred approach better defines the issues and the challenges. Coupled with this, observe the context of the people you are designing for so that all the factors that impact on a particular issue can be considered.

Make possible solutions visible through drawing, prototyping (which doesn't need to be expensive) so that meaningful iteration can take place.

With these iterations, involve the people who will benefit from the final outcome. The Helen Hamlyn Design Centre which is part of the Royal College of Art has a number of open access publications that provide guidance on this, including involving people with disabilities.

The truth is that it takes a concerted effort and focus to see it through. Here we give two examples of where it didn't work well for us at SJOG and where it did.

Community kickstart - when things don't go so well

In June 2019 we carried out a consultation with the local community where we run a community centre. This piggy-backed a family fun day and we were able to gather insights on what local people would want from the centre. The answers focused on support for young people and courses that would be easy to engage with. We'd discovered the needs of the community, although the sample was reasonably small with 62 people.

Armed with this, we took this and saw a funding opportunity aimed at supporting people over 30 to improve their mental health. The community centre is located in an area of poverty sandwiched between affluent areas of Hertfordshire. Based on this we developed a project called community kickstart. This had been successfully run in the north of England and so we assumed that the similar social economic make up would transfer to Hertfordshire.

We were successful in the securing the funding. However, in delivering the project we noticed that the local community was not engaged with the centre as much as we anticipated. A consultation on a family fun day had skewed the data we had collected. This made delivery difficult as engagement with the community was much more challenging. Not long after the project started, the Covid-19 pandemic hit and the community centre was closed. We were fortunate that the funders allowed us to reallocate the funding to support mental health of our colleagues.

What did we learn from this failure? Well, that we should have listened to our consultation. Provision for young people in the area is poor. That when developing the project specifically for the funding call, we should have had a focused engagement event with the community to shape our offer and specifically define the problem we were addressing. By doing this we would have been able to iterate on a previously successful service model to make it suitable for the local context. Lesson learned. This is why prototyping as much as possible as quickly and as cheaply as possible is key to launching successful new opportunities.

Magic space - when things do go well

Towards the end of 2019, SJOG's opportunities team had identified that sensory therapy for the people we support with learning disabilities and autism was difficult to access. At the same time, we had seen that new technology was being applied in the educational setting that created interactive virtual spaces that could be used to support pupils in their learning of a particular topic.

We set about exploring this in more detail to discover the problem. It was apparent that bespoke sensory therapy was not widely available but the concept of it could significantly benefit the people we are here to support. In December 2019 we carried out a review of the needs of 38 people in our care including wheelchair users, people with autism, complex needs, blind and hearing impairments.

Feedback on the benefits were that the personalisation offered by immersive sensory therapy was profound. Individualised sensory experiences would be created that could suit individual needs related to their care plans and target outcomes. This defined the challenge for us: to create a mobile immersive sensory therapy unit that could travel to people we support. We called this Magic Space.

Working in partnership with a technology provider we developed a prototype concept to two of our care homes for the people we support to trial the approach. We took qualitative feedback and used this to define our offer further. We also spoke to 31 internal stakeholders, ranging from trustees through to our support worker colleagues. Our support workers' detailed feedback fed into the concept development and how Magic Space was to be directly applied to care provision.

A further 14 external stakeholders were engaged. These ranged from university professors researching the area of health technology, through to nurses and allied health professionals who reviewed and commented on the concept in relation to current care provision and how this supplements and extends opportunities for these people.

From this we had the requirements for the sensory unit, a plan for the role out and a research programme that would evaluate the impact of the sensory unit for the people we support. In mid-2020 we secured £100K grant funding to deliver Magic Space to the people we support. In January 2021 it went live.

This was a great success. The process of going through the double diamond meant that all the thinking was done properly with the project considered in full. It involved colleagues from opportunities driving the process, from operations helping gather insights to define the problem and requirements, and from our support teams (finance and IT) to make it all happen. At the heart was a really good understanding of the problem that was being solved and the needs that were met through the solution. Ultimately it is this that meant that a compelling case for support.

Building a culture and approach to opportunities keeps an eye on the future and is one part to ensure the sustainability of a charity. Hopefully what we've shown is that innovation (should we call it that!?) is accessible. By applying a consistent method, such as design thinking, it can be structured into the core activities of an organisation.

Questions to ask yourself
- What is our biggest blocker to embracing innovation?
- If it is the perception of innovation, how can we reframe it to use the same process but in a more accessible way?

Reflection

Use the notion of innovation but think about how your colleagues would best respond to this- use the language of the charity.

Embrace the process of design thinking but make time to embed it in a way that isn't tokenistic.

Always start from the observing and finding out the needs of the people you are supporting.

Don't be afraid to scrap ideas and start again. Embrace iteration.

References

Baregheh, A., Rowley, J., & Sambrook, 5. (2009). Towards a multidisciplinary definition of innovation. Management decision.

Brown, T. (2008). Design thinking. Harvard business review, 86(6), 84.

Dyer, J.,Gregersen, H., &Christensen, C. M. (2011). The innovator's DNA. Boston, MA: Harvard Business Review Press. Kelley, T., & Kelley, D. (2012). Reclaim your creative confidence. Harvard business review, 90(12), 115-118.

Kahn, K. B. (2018). Understanding innovation. Business Horizons, 61(3), 453-460.

Framework for Innovation (2021). https://www.designcouncil.org.uk/news-opinion/what-framework-innovation-design-councils-evolved-double-diamond

Luchs, M. G. (2016). A brief introduction to design thinking. In M. G. Luchs, K. 5. Swam, & A. Griffin (Eds.), Design thinking. Hoboken NJ: John Wiley & Sons.

O'Bryan, M. (2013, November). Innovation: The most important and overused word in America. Wired Magazine. Available at https://www.wired.com/insights/2013/11/innovation-themost-important-and-overused-word-in-america/

Zhexembayeva, N. (2020). Stop calling it "innovation". Harvard business review.

Resources

Stickdorn, M., Schneider, J., Andrews, K., & Lawrence, A. (2011). This isservice design thinking: Basics, tools, cases (Vol. 1). Hoboken, NJ: Wiley.

Downe, L., (2020) Service Design,. https://good.services/ [accessed 23.8.2021]

Interaction Design Foundation: https://www.interaction-design.org/literature/topics/service-design [accessed 23.8.2021]

Design Council. Method for developing services: https://www.designcouncil.org.uk/sites/default/files/asset/document/Design%20methods%20for%20developing%20services.pdf [accessed 23.8.2021]

Managing yourself

How to be comfortable with not being truly accomplished

What you will find here:

- Embracing the imposter
- Be kind to yourself
- Be brave

Taking care of the care taker

All too often our attention is focused outwards. It's about our organisation, our colleagues and the people we are here to support, but if you are going to be effective in taking care of all of the things going on in your charity then you need to also take care of yourself.

I'm not talking about spa treatments or gym sessions (though both are good!) but where we all need to be better is on not being too hard on ourselves. You need to give yourself a break.

Running a charity is complicated, and along the way, if you are anything like me then you'll have doubts about whether you are on the right path, whether things are moving fast enough, whether you should be having a bigger impact, whether you are having too much of an impact and too quickly, or whether you are up to the task in hand. It's natural and healthy to question yourself, but moderation in all things.

No matter what role I've been in, I've always been uncertain as to whether I can do the job that I've been recruited to do. Now before I'm let loose in a role, I will have been through the interview process, made to jump through a series of hoops, undertaken a series of tests, and my past successes and experience will have been scrutinised. After all of these tests, and comparing me with others, a group of people have decided that I'm the right person to fulfil this role, but still I always have doubt going into a new role, and I think that's a good thing.

Embrace the imposter

It would be wrong of me to say that I love imposter syndrome, which is the belief that you don't belong and are not good enough to be doing what you are doing, but I do find it useful.

Let me explain. Like everyone else I keep expecting someone to pick up the phone and say, "Well, we worked out you really don't know what you are doing. You had a good run, but it's time to get your coat."

I tell myself that I shouldn't feel this way. I've been a chief executive for a number of years and worked for charities for 30 years. I've run programmes across the four nations of the UK, turned around charities that were failing and picked up a number of awards for the quality of the work that we do and how we do it, but there are days when I still feel like an imposter and that's ok with me because I am in excellent company.

Maya Angelou is quoted as saying:

> "I have written eleven books, but each time I think, uh oh, they're going to find me out."

I like this, this honesty, this natural vulnerability. The people I struggle to engage with are the people who present as knowing everything, being supremely confident and able to turn their hand to anything. It just smacks me as being a little false and lacking in self-awareness, but maybe it's not a front and there are people who are really like this?

It reminds me of Mr Darcy in Pride and Prejudice complaining about the overuse of the term 'accomplished' when applied to young ladies and that he knows of only six women who are accomplished.

> "A woman must have a thorough knowledge of music, singing, drawing, dancing, all the modern languages, to deserve the word; and besides all this, she must possess a certain something in her air and manner of walking, the tone of her voice, her address and expressions, or the word will be but half deserved and to all this she must yet add something more substantial, in the improvement of her mind by extensive reading."

Blimey!

Fittingly, Elizabeth Bennet replies that:

> "I am no longer surprised at your knowing only six accomplished women. I rather wonder now at your knowing any..... I never saw such a woman."

I love this dose of realism to counter the pompous ideal, but I have to admit that sometimes I fall foul of believing that everyone else is part of 'the accomplished'.

In my role I sometimes meet or sit on a panel with a group of other people who lead charities, businesses, or people in the political and the public sphere. There are times when I wonder if I'm there just to make up numbers, or because someone else has dropped out. I look around the table, or at the panel and see their reputations, and I see that they are accomplished rather than that they are people.

It's not a level playing field because whilst we know how we feel we only see the person they project. It comforts me to think that they live in their reality and are probably doing much the same thing looking at everyone else and working out whether they belong.

As I've spent more time in the charity sector, I've learnt more about it. It's huge and varied and I've learnt that as I know more, I'm also aware that there is more that I know I don't know. I know there are things that are unknowns (and that's before I get to the unknown unknowns).

My fear, when I sit on panels or go to meetings, is that the other people in the room know the things that I don't. That they know more than I do.

The reality is that they very well might, but more likely is that they just know different things. At the end of the day, they know what they know, and you know what you know. You know?

They might be more erudite, they might be better educated or more confident (which is different to more competent), but on these occasions I find it useful to focus on the fact that you are there for a reason. You have a job of work to do, and that if these people are really great then today is a fantastic opportunity to learn from them.

If you are new to an organisation then that feeling of not knowing things can be stifling. Relax, I can guarantee that on day seven in a role you will know more about the organisation that you work for, the way it works, the legislative framework it sits in, and the people that surround you, than you did on day one.

We learn, and the great thing is that we continue to learn throughout our lives.

Carole Dweck talks about a growth mindset and the idea of neuroplasticity; that is we can change, grow and learn throughout our life. You can teach an old dog new tricks, and the reason that you are in the role that you are in, is because you have continued to develop and learn.

If you were recruited into your role then someone thinks that you are worthy to be trusted. They believe that you won't break the organisation and that you might even make a success of it.

Hopefully, you took on this role as an opportunity to take the next step, to take on a fresh challenge. I say hopefully because I was once advised to never apply for a job that you know that you can do. It was good advice, stretch yourself, go with enough skills to make a reasonable fist of the role from day one, but leave space for some growth and personal development.

It's in this space, the area where you are growing your capacity and your confidence that you will feel like an imposter. Growth is uncomfortable, it would be easier to stay inside our shell and not risk not being good enough or failing, but that's a trick in its own right because that leads to complacency, stagnation and frustration.

We need to move, to occasionally stick our neck out because like the tortoise we only make progress when we do.

For me imposter syndrome helps me because it means that I'm always trying to be competent to do my job. I'm not sitting back with my feet on the desk, with my hands behind my head thinking 'Job done!', I'm always trying to help the charity better able to do what it does.

I've been told that I present as being confident, and sometimes I am, and sometimes less so. I know that I need to practice confidence. I once saw a t-shirt which said that 'Confidence is not a trait but a habit' (so it must be true).

As I've been doing this role longer, I've learnt that it's ok not to know stuff, and to say I don't know. I've learnt that it's ok not to have the answers, and it's ok not to be perfect - that person would be truly terrifying and as Elizabeth Bennett said, 'I never saw such a woman', nor should I add, a man either.

Be an informed consumer

For me the writing of this book has been about embracing my imposter. This is new to me and I can hear my imposter syndrome asking, "Should anyone listen to what I have to say?", and "Has the world really been waiting for a book from you?" and the answer to both of those are of course a resounding 'No'.

No one should listen to what I have to say, but they may choose to and there may be things in here that are helpful, as well as a whole load of information that you will jettison and never think of again.

What I hope is that in this book, you will find an honest account of what we have learnt over our years in the charity sector, but don't trust us blindly, evaluate and decide for yourself.

There is a lot of bunkum out there, stuff that is the modern day equivalent of snake oil, and so you'll need to use your faculties to determine what you believe in and what not to. For instance, the third Monday of January is apparently the most miserable day of the year, it even has its own title 'Blue Monday'.

It's miserable because it is part of the post-Christmas, post new year lull. The nights are still long and dark, and it's cold. Most people will have been paid before Christmas, so it's been a long time since our bank accounts have had an influx of cash, the cost of the revelry in the holiday period has now all been detailed in our credit card statements, and there's are still 10 days to go before we are paid.

The people behind Blue Monday calculated that it's the most miserable day of the year by using a mathematical formula that includes factors such as weather conditions, debt levels, our ability to pay, time since Christmas, time since failing our New Year's resolutions, low motivation and a feeling that we should but are not taking action.

The impressive looking formula is:

$((W+(D-d)) \times T'')/ (M \times N,)$

Where W = weather, d = debt, D = monthly salary, T = time since Christmas and so on.

Now I studied maths at university, I wasn't very good at it, but I'd guess that the equation is not real because it violates the fundamental property of dimensional homogeneity. It's a bit like asking 'Which is more, a centimetre or an hour?'.

Whilst it looks clever the equation, I believe that this was created for a travel company trying to encourage us to book holidays in January.

So why have I spent so long explaining something that I think is bunkum? Partly to say that we need to be careful of the measures that we believe in, partly to tell you that you are in charge of your own happiness rather than the marketing company, and partly to say that if you are in doubt about whether something is right, run it past someone that you trust.

This book has been written by us as a team. We've divvied up the chapters, some have a single author, some have been written by more than one of us, contributing bits to hopefully expound, enlighten and provide more context. All of the chapters have been read and reviewed by all of us, adding comments, supporting and challenging each other along the way. It's a better book because of it. We all need others, people we can turn to and say 'Well… ?'

Pace yourself

I run. Not fast, but I do run. I've run marathons and half marathons, 5ks, but I've settled on 10k as my preferred distance. It's far enough to feel like you've had a good run out, and even on my slowest days I'm out and back and in the shower within an hour.

There are days when I feel good and I run faster, and on the days when it's a bit of struggle I go a little slower and cut myself some slack. If I run a 10k in 55 minutes rather 50 minutes, in the big scheme of things, what does it matter?

I used to have a running buddy who was a big fan of trail running and he could be guaranteed to set a path that included running up big hills. I hated those hills because I used to try and keep my pace up, but as he said to me when faced with a hill it doesn't matter how slow you go up them, just keep going, don't stop and you'll still get to the top.

It's the same sentiment that my mum used to share with me when she said, 'Tuesday always follows Monday'. If it takes a little longer does it matter? Sometimes it's the pressure that we put on ourselves that makes our days more challenging.

It's trite to say that the running of a charity is a marathon rather than a sprint, but it's trite because it's true. This is a longer commitment, and there are times when you will be sorely tested and feel like you don't want to go on. Those are the points when you slow down, take a breath and keep going.

You'll get there but it will take time for you to feel like the charity is working as you want it to. In my first role as chief executive, I was four years in and into my second strategy before I felt that we were flying. We had the right people in place, people who were better than me at doing their job, they were all pulling in the same direction and doing things that I hadn't even thought were possible.

We spoke in the chapter on change that progress is less constantly forward and more like a meandering river, sometimes you are moving directly towards the sea. Sometimes it feels like you are barely making any progress forward at all. Give yourself a break, keep going you'll get there.

Be brave

We all have dark teatimes of the soul, times when we just feel that we might not have got it right, or when we are worrying about what comes next. We've covered already that Joe Strummer said that the future is unwritten. That uncertainty about what the future holds can be paralysing if we allow it to be.

When Seamus Heaney, the Irish poet was dying, he sent a text to his wife that contained just two words 'Noli Timere'. Not everyone could get away with sending their last words in a text in Latin without seeming pretentious, but Seamus Heaney had spent his life crafting words, and received a Nobel prize for his body of writing, so if anyone can carry this off then I think he can probably can.

'Noli Timere' means 'Don't be afraid' and it's been said that he was quoting from the bible, and this catholic turned agnostic may have been, after all it's the words that Mary was greeted with by the angel who told her she was going to have a baby.

If it was a quote at the point of death, it seems odd that Seamus Heaney should choose words associated with birth, but both birth and death are moments of transition, a change from one state to another, and all change is going from the known into the unknown, from the present into the future. The best that we can hope for is to embrace these.

We all have periods of uncertainty in our life, the first day of school, becoming a parent, relocating, taking on a new job, and we all feel it in the pit of our stomach, but time moves on and as it does it shows us that our fears are not realised, that the world continues to turn, and that Tuesday follows Monday.

Bouncebackability

Psychologists are getting quite excited by resilience. I've spoken earlier about the need to be robust, and have bucket loads of resolve, and whilst resilience is connected to both of these it's not quite the same this. The definition of resilience that I like is that it is the capacity to recover quickly from difficulties. It doesn't mean that you don't have challenges, or that you find things easy, but that when things don't work, you can recover.

I call this bouncebackability.

Warren Buffet who is one of the wealthiest people on the planet, made his money by taking organisations that were failing and making them well again. He talked about his ideal investment being in a sick company that was on the operating table but with a really good chance of recovery.

In 2014, the American psychological association published 'The Road to Resilience' which identified a series of factors that contributed to the ability to bounce back.

1. The ability to make plans and put those plans into action
2. Belief in one's own abilities
3. Communication and problem-solving skills
4. Self-control (managing strong impulses and feelings)

Which all sound like just the traits that we've spoken about through this book. Understanding the world as it is, putting in plans, realising 'You're it' and then engaging with the challenges that this presents.

What I think is missing from the American study is a sense of humour...(I'll just let that sit there!). We talk in SJOG about taking the work that we do seriously but not taking ourselves too seriously. LOLS and giggles are very important.

Whilst this wasn't covered in The Road to Resilience it was part of a Swiss study called, 'Humour as a character strength among the elderly'.

Ageing brings its own challenges and is the major cause of disability, but the happiest people in the study were those who used humour as a means of coping with the challenges of old age.

The final point on bouncebackability is that there are some protective factors that aren't all about you. You need someone who has your back and is on your side, someone who is important to you and to whom you are important. As we have mentioned more than once, running a charity is a team sport and you need buddies.

This chapter may be called Managing Yourself, but you don't need to do it all by yourself.

Resilience

In the chapter on People, we talk about our colleagues being complicated emotional beings. It's true, but what is also true is that so are you.

As the leader of your team, you'll be the one who sets the tempo of the work. You'll set the tone, and people will look to you for direction, reassurance, support and encouragement, but who do you turn to when you are having one of those days when you just don't feel 100%, when you feel like you could do with a cheerleader, someone who will turn to you and say "Yep, I know, but come on you can..."

We all need buddies, whether these are social buddies, a network of colleagues, family, or a mentor. Someone who we value, and who we believe has our best interests at heart. Someone who we can bounce ideas off, have a bit of a moan, and someone who will occasionally give us a figurative kick up the bum, and tell us to stop whining and get on with it.

When we were first talking about putting this book together, we talked about 'our team being of help to your team'.

We hope that you've found both practical support and affirmation that you are on the right track. We do hope that what is in here is of real help to you, and we are here to help so if you want to reach out, to ask questions or just bounce an idea off us then we'd love to hear from you.

And now that we've got this far, you need to put down the book and get on with it.

Reflection
- It's ok not to know everything.
- Noli Timere.

References

American Psychological Association. (2014). The Road to Resilience.

Ruch, W.; Proyer, R.T.; Weber, M. (2009). "Humor as a character strength among the elderly" (PDF). leitschrift flr Gerontologie und Geriatrie. 43 (1): 13-18. doi:10.1007/s00391-009-0090-0.PMID20012063.SIC/D25341461.

Werner, E.E. (1995). "Resilience in development". Current Directions in Psychological Science. 4 (3):81-85. doi:10.1111/1467- 8721.ep10772327. SICID 143879633.

Austin, J.Pride and prejudice

The Guardian (2013).Seamus Heaney's last words https://www.theguardian.com/books/2013/sep/02/seamus-heaney-last-words funeral#:-:text=His%20last%20words%20were%20%22in,'%22

Reach out

We benefit from a great senior team at SJOG, a group of people who came together regularly, can moan together and then get on with sorting things and making things better together. It's a great thing and if we can help then we will.

At the beginning we listed our contact details, and here they are again:

paulbott@sjog.org.uk

leannewelford@sjog.org.uk

lisaalcorn@sjog.org.uk

jamiemackrill@sjog.org.uk

Acknowledgements

This book is a collective work, so is it self-congratulatory to thank the team that wrote this book?

Thank you for all that has been achieved over the past years, for the way that it been done, and for all the wit and the collective wisdom. It's great to be part of this team.

Thanks have to go to Karen Gilroy for her work in turning our writings and diagrams into the beautiful object that you hold in your hands.

To all our colleagues, trustees and the people who we are here to serve, thank you. You make our community very special by living our values every day and it's a joy to work alongside you.

Thank you to Robert Nieri, Charity Partner at Shoosmiths, for taking the time to read and comment on an early draft.

Finally, we continue to be inspired by the example of our founder who said "Doing good, does you good." 450 years later we are still trying to do good and be of help.

All income from the sale of this book goes to further the work of SJOG, a charity registered in England and Wales.

Authors' bios

Paul Bott is Chief Executive of SJOG and has worked and volunteered in charitable organisations for the past 30 years. Paul was recognised as the Third Sector Leader of the year in 2021.

Dr Lisa Alcorn is SJOG's Chief Operating Officer. Lisa specialises in Autism and Positive Behaviour Support; work that has been recognised by the British Institute of Learning Disabilities PBS International Awards and the National Learning Disability and Autism Awards.

Dr Jamie Mackrill is SJOG's Chief Development Officer. Jamie lectured in human-centred design and human factors at Imperial College London and the Royal School of Art before moving into the charity sector to develop services, projects and platforms that meet the needs of the people we are here to support.

Leanne Welford is SJOG's Chief Finance Officer and Company Secretary. Leanne is a chartered accountant and holds an MBA. Leanne worked in the private sector before she moved to the charity sector and is passionate about making finance integral to achieving outcomes for the people we support. Leanne and SJOG's Finance Team were recognised as the Charity Finance Team of the Year 2021.